LOST IN
TRANSFORMATION

LOST IN
TRANSFORMATION

SOUTH AFRICA'S SEARCH FOR A NEW FUTURE SINCE 1986

SAMPIE TERREBLANCHE

Review
Publishing

KMM REVIEW PUBLISHING COMPANY
JOHANNESBURG

Published in 2012 by
KMM Review Publishing Company (PTY) Ltd
PO Box 782114, Sandton 2146

First impression 2012
Second impression 2012
Third impression 2015
Fourth impression 2018
Fifth impression 2020

ISBN 978-0-620-53725-4

Cover, design, typesetting and layout:
Brandon van Heerden, Johannesburg

Printing and binding:
Typo Printing

Contents

Contents

Glossary

AA	Affirmative Action
AAC	Anglo American Corporation
AEE	Afrikaner Economic Empowerment
ANC	African National Congress
AP	Affirmative Procurement
BAD	Bantu Affairs Department
BEE	Black Economic Empowerment
BEIC	British East India Company
BRICS	Brazil, Russia, India, China and South Africa
BWI	Bretton Woods Institutions
CBM	Consultative Business Movement
CEE	Commission for Employment Equity
CM	Chamber of Mines
CODESA	Convention for a Democratic South Africa
COSATU	Congress of South African Trade Unions
DP	Democratic Party
EEA	Employment Equity Act 55 of 1998
EIC	East Indian Company
EPG	Eminent Persons Group
EOI	Export Orientated Industrialisation
FDI	Foreign Direct Investment
FMF	Free Market Foundation
GATT	General Agreement on Tariffs and Trade
GDP	Gross Domestic Product
GEAR	Growth, Employment and Redistribution Strategy
IM	Independent Movement
IMF	international Monetary Fund
IP	Independent Party

ISI	Import-substituting industrialisation
JRC	Justice and Reconciliation Committee
MEC	Mineral Energy Complex
NAD	Native Affairs Department
NDP	National Development Plan
NDM	National Democratic Movement
NEC	National executive committee
NEM	Normative Economic Model
NP	National Party
NPA	National Planning Commission
OPEC	Organisation of Petroleum Exporting Countries
PDI	Previously Disadvantaged Individuals
PFP	Progressive Federal Party
PUI	Poverty, Unemployment and Inequality
RDP	Reconstruction and Development Programme
SALDRU	Southern Africa Labour and Development Research Unit
SANAC	South African Native Affairs Commission
SAP	South African Party
SDI	Strategic Defence Initiative
TAC	Treatment Action Campaign
TEC	Transitional executive council
TNCs	Transnational Corporations
TRC	Truth and Reconciliation Commission
UDF	United Democratic Front
VOC	Verenigde Oostindische Compagnie (Dutch East India Company)
WTA	White Triple Alliance
WTO	World Trade Organisation

Preface

The outstanding characteristic of South Africa, eighteen years after the transition of 1994, is the intensification of the country's social problems of poverty, unemployment and inequality (the PUI problem) among the poorest 50 per cent of the population – in other words, the majority of the black people. The interaction between poverty, unemployment and inequality has not only entrenched and aggravated the black majority's predicament, but has also intensified the burden of their deprivation. The intensification of the PUI problem can be ascribed partly to the co-option of South Africa as a satellite of the American-led neoliberal empire, and partly to the misguided and myopic policy initiatives of the ANC government. Ironically enough, the power and wealth of the white controlled capitalist sector was enhanced by its integration into the power structures of the American orientated neoliberal global economy.

By misgoverning South Africa over the past eighteen years, the ANC government has become trapped in a 'catch-22'. The PUI problem that was bequeathed to the ANC government by the apartheid regime in 1994 was already almost unsolvable. The ANC has proclaimed repeatedly that addressing the PUI problem is its highest priority. But this is only true in the rhetorical sense of the word. The policy measures implemented by the government over the past eighteen years have given strong preference to black elite formation and to promoting the interests of local and foreign corporations while it has shamelessly neglected the impoverished black majority. As a consequence, not only has the PUI problem become more severe – it is also much more unsolvable.

The ANC government is strongly inclined towards elite formation, towards corruption and towards pampering the interest of the capitalist elite, while it displays a conspicuous inability to govern South Africa with efficiency and fairness and to alleviate the predicament of the poor. This contradiction gives us reason to suspect that the downward spiral of the PUI problem will be perpetuated for at least another decade or two.

To liberate itself from the stranglehold of the 'catch-22' situation, the ANC government will have to become more efficient, less corrupt and orientated in a much friendlier way towards the impoverished black majority. But it is doubtful whether the ANC can liberate itself from its misguided priorities and its glaring inability to govern with *governance* and *fairness*.

SJ Terreblanche
Stellenbosch July 2012

Introduction

My book *A History of Inequality in South Africa: 1652-2002* was published in 2002. At that stage, the African National Congress (ANC) government had been in office for eight years. It is now ten years later, a momentous ten years, not only in South Africa but also worldwide. The United States became involved in two controversial wars – in Iraq and in Afghanistan – and, since 2008, has been experiencing the Great Recession, the most severe economic downturn since the Great Depression. Both the US and the Eurozone countries are confronted with unprecedented debt crises. The Great Recession and the debt crises have plunged the system of global capitalism and the ideology of market fundamentalism into crises of survival on both sides of the North Atlantic.

David Rothkopf wrote in *Time* magazine (30 January 2012) that 'today's contest is not so much between capitalism and another ideology, but between competing forms of capitalism. The financial crisis, growing inequality and faltering economic performance in the US have tarnished American 'leave it to the markets' capitalism, which is being challenged by 'capitalism with Chinese characteristics', eurocapitalism, 'democratic development capitalism' (as in India and Brazil), and even small-state entrepreneurial capitalism (as in Singapore, the United Arab Emirates and Israel). All these models favour a more significant role for the state in regulation and ownership of the control of assets.'

To look at the South African transformation in the early 1990s from the perspective of 2012, instead of from the perspective of 2002, makes an enormous difference. This new perspective enables me to make a radically new evaluation of Codesa and the secret negotiations that took place in the early 1990s, and also allows a radically new evaluation of South Africa's economy and the ANC government's performance over the past eighteen years.

In *A history of Inequality*, I described the transformation that took place in 1993/94 as an 'incomplete transformation' and asked what could be done to make it more 'complete'. I described it thus because in 2002 I was of the opinion that only the political dimension of our politico-economic system had changed – from white political dominance to an African-controlled democracy – while the economic dimension remained almost intact as a system of free-market capitalism. I realise today that this view was incorrect because the transformation of 1993/94 was indeed a complete transformation: both the political and the economic sides of our dual politico-economic system were changed quite radically in the first half of the 1990s. But the changes that took place were the wrong changes, and created a new politico-economic system that is operating dysfunctionally.

We could describe the economic dimension of the politico-economic system in place in South Africa from 1795 until 1994 as a British-oriented system of colonial and racial capitalism that mercilessly exploited the African part of the black population in particular – especially after the discovery of gold in 1886. The political side of our politico-economic system in place from 1795 until 1994 was made up of a great variety of white colonial governments that were conspicuously weak against the power of the capitalist corporations operating in the country and, especially after 1886, in the mining and energy sectors.

We could describe our post-apartheid politico-economic system as a neocolonial satellite of the American-led neoliberal global empire that systemically excludes the poorest part of the population from participating in the global economy. The political side of our new politico-economic system is also conspicuously weak in relation to the powerful position of global capitalism/corporatism and the American-led neoliberal global empire. The ANC government is in an obviously weak position, as its sovereignty was fairly seriously restricted by the conditionalities that were made applicable when our economy was integrated into the structures of global capitalism, as I make clear in Chapter Four.

In Chapter One, I explain why I am of the opinion that the transformation process started in 1986, and in Chapter Two I describe the emergence of the American-led neoliberal global empire from the early 1980s. Given that the South African economy has been Americanised to a large extent over the past eighteen years, it is important that we should have a clear perception of the rise – and the possible decline – of the 'American empire' and of global capitalism/corporatism, which has largely determined the destiny of South Africans since 1994.

In Chapter Three, I provide an overview of the politico-economic systems in place in South Africa from 1652 until 1994 to demonstrate that capitalist corporations were uninterruptedly in a dominant position, vis-à-vis a great variety of rather weak white colonial governments.

In Chapter Four, I describe the South African transformation process as it was orchestrated by the minerals energy complex (MEC) from 1986 onwards. In the secret negotiations that took place in the early 1990s on the future economic system of South Africa, the MEC and the American pressure groups – which also participated in the secret negotiations – jointly played a dominant role in outwitting the leadership core of the ANC to agree to the elite compromise of 1993.[1] This compromise spelled out the conditionalities that would be applicable to the ANC government. Before the elite compromise was agreed upon, the MEC and the American pressure groups made hyper-optimistic promises of how economically advantageous it would be for South Africa if it were to become integrated into the structure of global capitalism/ corporatism and if the ANC (an erstwhile socialist organisation) should accept the ideologies of neoliberal globalism and market fundamentalism. I describe how the ANC orchestrated the prelude to the transformation process at the end of the 1980s and the secret negotiations that took place at the Development Bank of Southern Africa that led to the Americanisation of the South African economy; and I assess the weaknesses of South Africa's constitutional democracy, and the weaknesses of the ANC government, over the past eighteen years.

Chapter Five concentrates on the phenomenon of 'unfree black labour', which has been a permanent part of South Africa's economic history since 1652 and is destined to remain a defining characteristic of the South African labour landscape for decades to come. The ANC government used its affirmative action policy in the public and semi-public sectors to solve the unfree black labour problem (or the unemployment problem) by 'transforming' the public sector too quickly from an Afrikaner-oriented to an African-oriented sector. Unfortunately, the educational and skills levels of Africans were at such low levels, after more than 300 years of educational discrimination, that such rapid Africanisation of the public sector led to a collapse in the efficiency and the effectiveness of service delivery – especially at the second and third levels of government. This myopic policy, aimed at creating a black elite artificially, has merely perpetuated the phenomenon of unfree black labour as the level of unemployment continues to rise.

In Chapter Six, I discuss the intensification of South Africa's social problems: poverty, unemployment and inequality (the PUI problem), an intensification which can be ascribed partly to the integration of the economy into the structure of global capitalism/ corporatism, and partly to the misguided and short-sighted policy initiatives launched by the ANC government within the environment of neoliberal globalism, market fundamentalism and free trade policies.

In Chapter Seven, I speculate on the development path of the South African economy over the next eighteen years, until 2030, and try to establish whether the fairytale optimism displayed in the National Development Plan of the National Planning Commission is the more likely development path, or whether my pessimistic scenario that the downward trend of the PUI problem, experienced over the past forty years, will be that which continues over the next eighteen years.

In Chapter Eight, I lament the many things that went wrong during the transformation process from 1986 until 2012. It presents a rather bleak picture, and one wonders whether the ANC can be shocked into mending its errant ways over the next eighteen years.

chapter one

Why was 1986 the real turning point in South Africa's transformation?

The year 1986 was the real turning point in South Africa's democratic transformation. This twenty-five year transformation was not an isolated event but part of a major reconfiguration of the world's power constellation that was institutionalised after the Second World War. The South African transformation was not the result of the end of the Cold War. Rather, the fall of apartheid and the fall of the Soviet Union were separate but interrelated consequences of this major global reconfiguration of power in the decades after 1980 and in which the United States played a leading role.

The crisis in Western Europe after the Second World War created the opportunity for the US to launch the American-led social democratic empire in Western Europe. This led to the prosperous golden age of social democratic capitalism in the Western world that lasted until the 1970s, when the US experienced a crisis that weakened its position of power and prestige vis-à-vis the second and the third worlds. It was a crisis that – together with the techno-logical revolution brought about by electronic informatics in the US and the financialisation of the American economy through excessive money creation by the US in the 1970s (after the collapse of the original Bretton Woods system) – made it possible for the US to launch the American-led neoliberal empire in the early 1980s.

Nobody can doubt that the ending of the Cold War was beneficial. The important question – from a South African point of view – is whether the transformation that occurred in South Africa from 1986 was a good or a bad transformation. On the one hand, it was undoubtedly a good transformation as South Africa got rid of the immoral and inhuman apartheid regime. But what has been put in the place of apartheid is not necessarily good, and in many aspects it is rather bad. In this book I am revisiting the relevant events that took place in the world and in South Africa since 1986 from the perspective of 2012. With the knowledge of hindsight, I will try to put together a balanced evaluation of the qualitative nature of the transformation to determine the appropriateness of the politico-economic system that has succeeded that of white political dominance and racial capitalism which had been in place in South Africa since the early twentieth century.

My choice of 1986 as an important turning point in the history of the world and of South Africa is not an arbitrary one. At the end of 1986, the power constellations in the world – internationally and in South Africa – were to a high degree still as they had become institutionalised in the years immediately after the Second World War. In terms of global interstate relations, Cold War relations were still very much as they had crystallised in 1947. The US was still the hegemonic country in the free West and the Soviet Union was still the dominant country in the communist bloc. The ideological rivalry and the arms race between the two superpowers were still in full swing and the two superpowers were still regarded as incommensurable. Perhaps the most important international event in the forty years after the Second World War was the comprehensive decolonisation of erstwhile Western colonies. The independent countries of the third world organised themselves into the Group of 77 at the United Nations and participated in the ideological warfare between the two superpowers by playing them off against each other – especially on issues of anti-colonialism and of apartheid, which was regarded by the second and the third worlds as a perpetuation of Western colonialism and racism (or as 'colonialism of a special type').

In 1986, four important events occurred that not only put relations between the first, the second and the third worlds on new trajectories, but specifically also the relationship between South Africa and the rest of the world. These four events were: first, the explosion at the Chernobyl nuclear power plant in the Soviet Union on 26 April 1986; second, the comprehensive state of emergency declared by the apartheid government on 12 June 1986; third, the enactment of the Comprehensive Anti-Apartheid Act by the American Congress in early October 1986, four months after President Ronald Reagan vetoed the anti-apartheid legislation; and fourth, the summit conference that took place between President Reagan and Mikhail Gorbachev on 11-12 October near Reykjavik in Iceland.

Chernobyl: 26 April 1986

The Chernobyl disaster was an accident at a nuclear power plant in the Ukraine, in the Soviet Union. The explosion released into the atmosphere large quantities of radioactive material, which spread over much of the western part of the Soviet Union and northern Europe. It was the worst nuclear accident in history and an enormous embarrassment for the Soviet Union, raising serious doubts about the standard of the Soviet Union's nuclear technology and the standard of Soviet technology in general.

I visited Moscow in 1990. During my visit my hosts taught me the Russian word *pokazhuka*. It means lies, official lies and even more official lies. According to my hosts, this word was used to describe the nature of Leonid Brezhnev's period as president of the Soviet Union from 1964 until 1982. Brezhnev used *pokazhuka* to deceive the Soviet population into believing that the communist system was highly efficient and that the Soviet planners were succeeding in attaining all their planning targets. In reality, the Brezhnev period was a disastrous one in which the structural inefficiency of the centrally-led communist planning system led to widespread retrogression and misery in the Soviet Union.

Mikhail Gorbachev became general secretary of the Communist Party of the Soviet Union in 1985. Because of the *pokazhuka* propaganda that, metaphorically speaking, pervaded the Soviet Union like a thick cloud, it was not possible for Gorbachev to immediately see how feeble and how backward socio-economic conditions were in the Soviet Union after the Brezhnev period. But when the Chernobyl nuclear power plant exploded in 1986 it radiated, again metaphorically speaking, so much heat that it melted away the *pokazhuka* cloud and enabled Gorbachev to realise how badly the Soviet Union had regressed and how much it needed to cooperate with the Western world.

South Africa's comprehensive state of emergency: 12 June 1986

The struggle against the apartheid regime started with strikes by African workers in Durban in 1973 that were organised by illegal black trade unions. It intensified with the revolt of the Soweto students in 1976. On 20 August 1983, the United Democratic Front (UDF) was launched by the delegates of 565 anti-apartheid organisations and with prominent churchmen as the leaders. The UDF turned out to be a very effective internal organisation in the struggle against apartheid. The Congress of South African Trade Unions (Cosatu) was formed in December 1985 as part of the Tripartite Alliance with the ANC and the SA Communist Party (SACP).

To protect the apartheid regime against the upsurge of political violence in the mid 1980s, the South African government declared a comprehensive state of emergency on 12 June 1986. From then on, South Africa was governed by military and police generals known as the securocrats. Establishing this securocratic government at the end of the 1980s was a desperate attempt to prolong the lifespan of the apartheid regime. But in spite of terrible measures (which included illegal and immoral emergency measures) the securocrats increasingly lost control over the black townships. By 1989 the security situation in South Africa had become extremely precarious, and by 1990 the apartheid regime had no choice – under mounting internal and external pressure – but to agree to negotiate the terms of a new dispensation with the ANC.

The Comprehensive Anti-Apartheid Act of the American Congress: October 1986

After the Sharpeville massacre of 21 March 1960, foreign countries started to institute sanctions against the apartheid regime. In the 1960s, the United Nation introduced military sanctions, while several countries started to isolate South Africa by means of sanctions and disinvestment policies. Amid these escalating sanctions, the South African government enjoyed the support of Western governments until the early 1980s – especially from the right-wing governments of UK Prime Minister Margaret Thatcher and US President Ronald Reagan, both of whom used the argument that sanctions and disinvestment policies against South Africa would harm black people and increase their destitution. When the Comprehensive Anti-Apartheid Act was accepted by the American Congress early in 1986, President Reagan used his presidential veto to prevent the legislation from becoming law – but four months later Congress decided, with a large majority, to override Reagan's veto, the first time in the twentieth century that a president's foreign policy veto was set aside.

With the Comprehensive Anti-Apartheid Act of 1986, the foreign campaign to institute sanctions, boycotts and disinvestment policies against South Africa reached a zenith. The symbolic importance of the American Act was tremendous and enabled the disinvestment campaigns of the United States, and of many other countries, to achieve critical mass. Almost all the American universities withdrew their investments in corporations operating in South Africa. Many corporations themselves divested. The net capital flight from South Africa increased sharply in 1986, and triggered a dramatic

11

decline in the international exchange of the South African currency.

As the sanctions, boycotts and disinvestment measures of foreign countries directed against the apartheid regime escalated dramatically at the end of the 1980s, they created a grave crisis for the corporate sector in South Africa. This sector's profitability was seriously threatened not only by the sanctions and the disinvestment policies, but also by social unrest and the industrial action of black trade unions. The government implemented all kinds of strategies in a desperate attempt to restore the profitability of the corporate sector, but as none of these strategies succeeded, the corporate sector became increasingly convinced that the apartheid regime could not survive and ought to be abolished. In the final years of the decade, combined Afrikaner and English business became a strong pressure group for radical transformation in South Africa. This pressure from the corporate sector was orchestrated by the mineral energy complex, the MEC.

The Summit in Reykjavik between Reagan and Gorbachev: 11-12 October 1986

Shortly after his inauguration in 1981, President Reagan described the Soviet Union as an 'evil empire' and started to increase US military spending quite dramatically.[2] It is rather ironic, then, that it was the several summits that took place between Reagan and Gorbachev which exerted such drastic pressure for change in world history.[3]

The meeting in Reykjavik in 1986 between Reagan and Gorbachev was mainly about the reduction of intermediate-range nuclear weapons in Europe. While they were discussing the United States Strategic Defence Initiative (SDI, or the 'Star Wars' programme), the ability of the US to launch a supercomputer microchip military revolution was revealed to Gorbachev. When he was confronted with this military revolution, Gorbachev immediately realised the immense technological underdevelopment of the Soviet Union in comparison with the US.

According to Ulf Hedetoft (in Streeter, 2009) Gorbachev realised at Reykjavik that the two superpowers were 'simply beyond comparison in terms of political, economic, or ideological structure, but, more importantly, [also] with respect to economic, political, technological, and military power'. Hedetoft continues:

> The Reykjavik [moment] ... symbolically crystallises ... all of the systematic, pragmatic endeavours of the United States to achieve global *supremacy* and all of the illusionary policies of the USSR to catch up with and be recognised by its ideological adversary. This moment points irrevocably forward towards the pivotal turning point [in the Cold War] ... and the abdication of the Soviet Union from the aspirations it once harboured for (equal) superpower status [with the United States]

The abdication of the Soviet Union from its aspirations to be an equal superpower implied that after Chernobyl and Reykjavik Gorbachev had no choice but to abandon the Brezhnev doctrine of 1968 – that is, the right of the Soviet Union to maintain control in its east European sphere of influence. When Gorbachev dropped the Soviet Union's superpower aspirations, he also had no choice but to abandon the military and financial support the Soviet Union was giving to several militia groups in 'proxy wars' to expand Soviet influence. Gorbachev told Reagan at Reykjavik that he wanted to scale down the Soviet Union's involvement in regional conflicts. After the events in Chernobyl and Reykjavik, Gorbachev yet again had no choice but to inform the ANC in exile that the Soviet Union no longer had the inclination or the ability to support it in its military struggle against the apartheid regime in South Africa.

After Reykjavik, the Soviet Union put pressure on the ANC in exile to seek a negotiated settlement in South Africa, and after the enactment of the Comprehensive Anti-Apartheid Act of 1986 the US and other Western countries strongly increased their pressure on the apartheid regime to, similarly, negotiate a solution to the apartheid problem. It is quite remarkable that pressure on the ANC to seek a negotiated solution came in 1986 from Moscow, and in the same year South Africa's white government was pressurised to do the same by Washington.

After that, several South African groups became involved with the ANC in discussions about a possible negotiated solution. In July 1987, a South African delegation under the leadership of Dr Frederick van Zyl Slabbert and Dr Alex Boraine held discussions with the ANC in Dakar, Senegal. From October 1987 to February 1990 a group of Afrikaner academics – including Professors Willie Esterhuizen, Sampie Terreblanche, Willem de Klerk and Marinus Wiechers – were involved in seven clandestine meetings with ANC leaders Thabo Mbeki, Jacob Zuma, Aziz Pahad and many others. These 'talks-about-talks' were held mostly at the Mells Park estate near Bath in Britain. At the time we were not aware that the ANC was under Soviet pressure to seek a negotiated settlement, and we were also not aware that serious disagreement had erupted in the ANC leadership core about the advisability of seeking a negotiated and diplomatic solution with the apartheid regime. Thabo Mbeki was very charming and intellectually impressive during our informal 'talks-about-talks'. With hindsight, I realise that he must have been under immense pressure within the ANC to attain positive results in his rapprochement with Afrikaner academics. At the end of the 1980s, several meetings between other South African groups – such as the business sector and sports and women's groups – also took place with the ANC, mainly in Lusaka.

During the subsequent summits that took place between Reagan and Gorbachev in 1987 and 1988, a relationship of cooperation and reciprocal trust developed between them. They reached agreement that all the Great Powers – including the Soviet Union – would *strive* together to find negotiated and diplomatic solutions for all the important flashpoints in the world. The flashpoints they identified were the Namibia-Angola-Cuba problem, the South African apartheid problem, the conflicts between Israel and Palestine and between India and Pakistan, and the problems in Northern Ireland, Iran and North Korea.[4]

After Reagan and Gorbachev reached agreement that the leaders of the Great Powers would seek a diplomatic solution for the South African problem, they decided that the British prime minister, Margaret Thatcher, was in the best position to convince the South African government to enter into negotiations with the ANC. Although Britain was no longer as powerful as it had been, it was still in a key position because of its relationship with South Africa, a former British colony. The levels of Britain's trade with, and investments in, South Africa exceeded those of all other countries. Britain was also the only one of the major powers that had not instituted a sanctions and disinvestment policy against South Africa.

In 1986, Thatcher took the initiative of sending the Eminent Persons Group (EPG) to South Africa, and in April of that year it looked as if it might be possible for the EPG to reach agreement with the government on the issue of negotiations with the ANC. But on 15 May President PW Botha unexpectedly rejected the proposals of the EPG. Thatcher was furious and was not prepared to negotiate with Botha again.

After PW Botha had a stroke in January 1989, FW de Klerk was elected as leader of the National Party. Thatcher invited him for discussions in London. During their meeting on 23 June 1989, she told De Klerk – on behalf of all the leaders of the Great Powers – that she could no longer perpetuate her non-sanctions policy, that she wanted Nelson Mandela to be released before the end of 1989, and that negotiations should start between the South African government and the ANC as soon as possible.

I met the author Anthony Sampson at the British Embassy in Cape Town on the day that Nelson Mandela was released on 11 February 1990. Later, in May 1990, he told me in London how important the meeting on 23 June 1989 between Thatcher and De Klerk had been. He also told me that when the correspondence between Thatcher and De Klerk during the second half of 1989 was published, the role that Reagan, Gorbachev and Thatcher played in bringing the NP government and the ANC to the negotiating table would be made clear.

The emergence of the American-Led Neoliberal Global Empire in the 1980s

America's imperial endeavours until the Second World War

The Americans have not been prepared – at least, not until recently – to acknowledge that the US has become an imperium. During the Cold War the concepts of empire and imperialism had negative connotations in accordance with Lenin's theory, and during those years Americans looked at the position of the US in the world as one of primacy, leadership and hegemony. It is possible, however, to put forward arguments that America's imperialism does have a historic lifespan of almost 200 years. During the nineteenth century the original thirteen colonies – which had united to form the United States of America at the end of the War of Independence – did more than their fair share of land-grabbing. The United States bought additional territory very cheaply from Spain, France and Russia, militarily conquered large parts of Mexican and Spanish territories in the nineteenth century, and nearly eliminated the three million Indo-Americans in unprovoked military operations. From 1870 to 1940, the US was involved – indirectly and informally – in empire-building in Latin America behind the shield of the Monroe Doctrine. These doubtful actions were legitimised in terms of the semi-religious notion of America's Manifest Destiny.

The US experienced remarkable economic progress in the fifty years after the Civil War. Its share of the world's manufacturing output increased from 14,7 per cent in 1870 to 32 per cent in 1913 (Bairoch,1982 table 10). The direct involvement of the United States in the First World War was short but decisive. While the US had been heavily in debt to Europe before the war, it became a strong credit-providing country afterwards and hence benefitted hugely. The stimulus that the American economy experienced during the First World War continued after the war and enabled the US to maintain great prosperity and a high economic growth rate during the 'roaring twenties'.

The Great Depression (1929-1933) was a huge setback for the US. And, later, the US became more comprehensively embroiled in the Second World War than in the First World War. While the Second World War was even more destructive for the other countries involved than the First World War had been, it was even more beneficial to the US. During the Second World War, the US economy grew at a rate of roughly 10 per cent per annum – faster than ever before or ever since. From 1940 to 1953, industrial expansion in the US rose at a rate of over 15 per cent a year, and its share of total world manufacturing increased to 44,7 per cent in 1953 (Bairoch, 1982).

In the first three decades of the twentieth century, the US concentrated on mass production by making the principles of Fordism and Taylorism applicable to production and increasing the productivity of industrial labour. During the 1920s, the total production of agricultural and industrial output increased at such a rapid pace that Americans became increasingly concerned about the availability of markets – domestically and externally – in which it could sell or dump its surplus industrial and agricultural products. This concern of the 1920s became a deep-seated obsession during the depressed 1930s: that American production capacity had become too big and that the US would indeed be chronically haunted by 'over-production and over-capacity', and there was a sense that drastic measures would have to be taken to address these problems. Two such measures were implemented in the 1920s and 1930s to find solutions for the problem of the reputedly chronic tendency towards 'over-production and over-capacity'. They proved to be pointers towards the pattern of American empire-building in the second half of the twentieth century.

The first measure was to empower transnational corporations (TNCs) to infiltrate Latin America (and, in due course, other countries) in search of new investment opportunities and to open up markets in which the surplus industrial and agricultural products could be sold. The second measure was to launch aggressive advertising and marketing programmes to convince Americans to save less and spend more on consumer goods. Through these attempts to convince the American public to embrace the mass consumer society, the phenomenon of consumerism was born.

When the institution of transnational corporations and the phenomenon of consumerism emerged in the early twentieth century, nobody could have predicted the dominant role that corporatism and consumerism were destined to play in American capitalism and in American empire-building. The rise of transnational American corporations and of American consumerism were typically American, but these phenomena were foreign to Western Europe at the time.

The middle class in the US in the early twentieth century, like the British in the nineteenth century, was very much inclined to save a large portion of its income to become members of a rentier, or property-owning, class. It was not easy to convince them that it was in their individual and in their country's economic interests to spend as large a portion of their income as possible on consumer goods. The Americans were inclined towards principles of frugality in accordance with the moral convictions of the Puritans and it was also not easy to convince them to forsake their Judeo-Christian thriftiness. Consequently, it was necessary for the business sector to launch a massive propaganda campaign for American consumers, and from the early twentieth century the advertising (or consumerist) industry became an integral part of modern capitalism, and also one of the largest industries in the US and in other Western countries. With the acceptance of consumerism over and above rentiership (through savings), American capitalism experienced a radical meta-morphosis from the British capitalism of the nineteenth century. In the American economy of the twentieth century, US corporations increasingly became transnational corporations. At the same time as they became increasingly involved in the production of large quantities of consumer goods they were also engaged in propaganda campaigns to convince consumers – local and foreign – to satisfy not only their rational needs but also their artificially created desires.

The consumer revolution that took place during the early twentieth century changed the character and the dynamics of capitalism forever – first in the US and in due course in the rest of the world. Since then the advertising industry has, with the aid of the mass media – and with all the seductiveness of consumerism – no longer been selling goods to customers, but 'happiness' to consumers, who are assumed never to be satisfied or replete. The export of the consumerist revolution from the US to Europe (also a high-income economy) made sense. But to export the high-consumption economy, and consumerism, to the global South – where per capita income since 1950 has always been less than 20 per cent of the per capita income of the global North – was pure madness. It intensified the destitution of billions of people in the global South.

The American-led social democratic empire in Europe after the Second World War

Because of the poor socio-economic and the politico-ideological conditions in Western Europe after the Second World War, the US took on the responsibility of 'rescuing' Western Europe not only from its economic predicament but also from the communist threat – and the only way the US could 'rescue' Western Europe in the post-war era was to integrate it as an informal 'colony' of the American empire.[5] Although there could have been no doubt about the imperial ambitions of the US at the time, the Americanisation of Western Europe in the post-war period happened with such a light touch that it is possible to claim that after 1947 Western Europe became part of an American 'empire' by invitation and by consensus (see Lundestad, 2004; Maier, 2006). Although it may sound strange, there can be no doubt that Western Europe was culturally and economically Americanised during the third quarter of the twentieth century (see De Gracia, 2005). In contrast to European empire-building in the global South, the American empire-building in Western Europe during the third quarter of the twentieth century was not exploitative, but supportive. Nonetheless, it brought about such a thorough Americanisation of Europe that its impact was regarded in some cultural circles in Europe in rather negative terms.

In the years after the Second World War, Western countries reached consensus on two social democratic contracts: a domestic social democratic consensus to create greater social justice and social stability in the domestic affairs of all the capitalist countries in the West; and an international social democratic consensus to stabilise the capital flows and the economic relationships between Western capitalist countries. In this way, an American-led social democratic empire came into being in the Western world, laying the foundation for the prosperous Golden Age of social democratic capitalism that stretched from 1950 to 1973. The support given by the US to its informal 'colony' in Europe was so generous that the economic growth of Western Europe was higher from 1950 until 1973 than that of the United States itself.

The Marshall Plan of 1948 played a key role in integrating Western Europe as part of the American social democratic empire.[6] The importance of the conditionalities attached to the Marshall Plan was that the recipient countries should not only allow American-domiciled transnational corporations (TNCs) to operate freely in those countries, but should also grant them all the privileges that were available to domestic corporations. These conditionalities led

21

to considerable growth in the number of American and European TNCs in the free West and strengthened their roles, and these same conditionalities were later also made applicable to countries in the global South.

It was not easy for the Americans to convince Western Europe of the alleged merits of consumerism and a mass consumer society. In many Western European countries – but especially in France – people regarded American mass consumer culture with suspicion and as an expression of the vulgar materialist culture that had developed in the US. They could not, however, dispute the fact that the US had experienced such astonishing economic growth since 1870 that its citizens were able to maintain much higher living standards than those of Europe.

The United States crisis in the 1970s and the emergence of the American-led neoliberal global empire in the 1980s

At the end of the 1960s, the post-war boom came to an end and the US experienced not only fiscal and trade problems, but also a series of events that injured its power and prestige. Intolerably high government spending on defence and on infrastructural development during the 1950s, and increased social spending in the 1960s (after the enactment of President Johnson's Great Society legislation in 1965), together with the escalating spending on the Vietnam war, led to serious fiscal and financial problems in the US. The economic problems experienced by the US from 1968 until the early 1980s could be regarded as the result of 'imperial overstretch', as the country's commitment to public expenditure became so great that it had an impact on the continued productive vigour of the private sector.

At the end of the 1960s, the US was also confronted with serious social crises. The Civil Rights Movement that started in 1955 reached its zenith in 1968. The student unrest in 1969 against the

Vietnam war and the military-industrial complex shocked the country. The US ultimately lost the Vietnam war. In 1973, the US suffered heavy setbacks in the war between Egypt and Israel. During this war OPEC increased the price of oil steeply, which led in turn to worldwide stagflation in the 1970s: sharply reduced rates of realeconomic growth, combined with high inflation rates and rising unemployment. The US experienced four relatively severe recessions from the late 1960s to the early 1980s. When taxation was increased in the 1970s to pay for unemployment insurance, there were tax revolts. At the same time, the hegemony of the US was harmed by the accession of China to the Security Council (1971), the Portuguese defeat in Africa (1974), the Iranian Revolution (1979) and the Soviet Unions invasion of Afghanistan (1980). American international power and prestige were also seriously diminished by the Watergate scandal (1972/74).[7]

When European countries were not prepared to appreciate their currencies to improve the international competitiveness of the US, President Nixon abandoned the fixed gold-dollar exchange standard unilaterally in 1971. This devaluation of the dollar provided the US government and businesses with major competitive advantages for a short period in the escalating inter-capitalist struggle over the world's markets for industrial inputs and outputs. After the fixed gold-dollar exchange standard was abandoned (and with it the original Bretton Woods system of 1944), the US also started to create large amounts of additional money and continued to increase the money supply exponentially during the 1970s in spite of the fact that this money 'explosion' led to rising costs, to new risks and uncertainties, and to chronic stagflation. Only a fraction of the newly created liquidity found its way into new trade and production – most of it turned into petrodollars and eurodollars and were used for speculation in money markets. The sharp increase in the money supply in the 1970s led to a quick accumulation of financial assets:

this was the beginning of the financialisation of the global economy that has continued over the past forty years (see Arrighi, 1994).

The financialisation of the global economy made a substantial contribution to the process of globalisation under the leadership of the US. It led to large-scale speculation on global money and foreign exchange markets – something that had been discouraged and strictly regulated at the Bretton Woods conference of 1944 at the request of Keynes. After the original Bretton Woods system was abolished by Nixon in 1971, the world returned to global financial speculation as had happened in the late nineteenth and early twentieth centuries, but on a much larger scale.[8] Although financialisation of the global economy was very profitable and enhanced global intercommitment, it also made the world economy much more vulnerable, and since the 1980s the world has experienced several financial crises (with the Great Recession 2008-2012 as the most severe), not only of the international financial system, but also of the neoliberal capitalist system. The excessive speculation on global financial markets has done serious harm to the status of American-orientated global capitalism.

An important consequence of this financialisation of the world economy was that it facilitated the relocation of industrial production from the West to the global South, as well as the replacement of import substitution industrialisation (ISI) in the South with export-orientated industrialism (EOI). The US regarded the shift towards EOI in the Southern world in the 1970s with great apprehension and as an indication that it was losing its control of the global flow of industrial capital. In the latter part of the 1970s, the US attempted to regain control over transnationalised capital by financial means (the sharp increase of global liquidity) and by legal means. Both attempts failed dismally.

The Western world had succeeded in monopolising the process of industrialisation for 200 years, from 1770 until 1970, during which time a great divergence developed between the per capita incomes of the West and the South. When industrialisation started in Britain around 1770, the West's share of total world industrialisation was 20 per cent, while the share of the global South (excluding Russia and Japan) was 70 per cent. Two hundred years later, in 1973, the West's share was 60 per cent, while the share of the global South (excluding Japan and the Soviet Union) declined to only 10 per cent (Bairoch, 1982; Bairoch, 1993). During the 200 years in which the West came to dominate industrialisation and the global South became deindustrialised (or remained unindustrialised), the per capita income of the global South, as a percentage of the per capita income of the West, declined from 50 per cent in 1770 to 18,4 per cent in 1973 (Maddison, 2007).

When it became clear in the early 1980s that neither 'structural globalisation' (through the post-war technological revolution) nor 'financial globalisation' (through the sharp increase of euro-dollars and petrodollars) could re-establish American control of the flow of industrial capital, the powerful American TNCs persuaded Reagan to launch the neoliberal counter-revolution. This counter-revolution could be regarded as an ideological or neoliberal *coup d'état* and as an almost desperate attempt by the US to regain control over American transnational capital and the process of industrialisation. With this (ideological) *coup d'état*, the US orchestrated a power shift in favour of itself and other Western countries. The American neoliberal counter-revolution has also been advantageous over the past thirty years to those Southern countries that became industrialised with Western support. The emergence of the American-led neoliberal empire in the early 1980s, however, was very much to the detriment of those Southern countries that were heavily indebted and that had also not been supported by Western TNCs to become industrialised.

The American-led neoliberal empire and the bifurcation between industrialising and non-industrialising countries in the South

When Reagan launched the neoliberal counter-revolution in the early 1980s he conceded to the request of the American-domiciled TNCs and IMIs to be empowered to infiltrate Southern countries with greater aggressiveness and with greater freedom. An important implication of Reagan's deregulation, liberalisation and privatisation measures was that TNCs became able to enter into 'partnership industrialisation' with 'corporations' in Southern countries to ensure that the US did not lose control over EOI in these countries. Since the early 1980s, Western TNCs have entered into partnership industrialisation with some Southern countries, but not with those that were highly indebted.

When Reagan was convinced by the TNCs to abolish almost all the regulations enacted by the American Congress since the Great Depression and during the social democratic consensus after the Second World War, a kind of regulatory vacuum was created for the TNCs. They were now 'free' and 'empowered' to act – especially in the global South – as they pleased. With his neoliberal counter-revolution, President Reagan created a new 'Wild West', a 'lawless' world in which the TNCs could, for all practical purposes, not be held accountable for their malpractices. In this way the global economy was 'criminalised' by the neoliberal counter-revolution, by which labour became as powerless against capital as was the case in the nineteenth century.

Western TNCs were empowered to enter into partnership-industrialisation with those Southern countries that were not heavily indebted, that had already experienced some ISI and EOI, and that had a reasonably educated and disciplined workforce at their disposal which made it possible to produce products at unit labour costs competitive in global markets. In these West-South partner-ships, the Western TNCs supplied some foreign direct investment

(FDI) and modern Western technology (protected by the rules of the World Trade Organisation). These partnerships were advantageous for the West (which earned a large imperial dividend) and for the industrialising Southern countries that attained higher economic growth rates and higher levels of employment. In the case of China and India, many of the products produced through partnership industrialisation were exported relatively cheaply to the West (and especially to the US), while China and India bought American bonds to enable the US to import the products from Asia.

Western TNCs, however, were not prepared to enter into partnership industrialisation with those Southern countries that were heavily indebted, that did not have meaningful experience of ISI and EOI, and did not have a reasonably educated and disciplined labour force. It would not have been possible under such circumstances to produce at unit labour costs that would be competitive in global markets. Western TNCs did, however, channel some FDI to these Southern countries for purposes of mineral exploitation.

To address the high level of indebtedness of these non-industrialising Southern countries, the Bretton Woods Institutions made structural adjustment programmes (SAPs) applicable to coerce these countries into developing an export capacity that would enable them to repay at least part of their huge foreign debts. The SAPs discouraged infrastructural development and also discouraged the accumulation of social capital in these Southern countries. The level of the brain drain from these countries to the West has been at an alarmingly high level over the past thirty years. The non-industrialising countries in the global South have become considerably poorer since 1980; their per capita income as a percentage of the per capita income of the West declined fairly sharply after 1973. The criminalisation of the global economy happened very much to their detriment.

Those Southern countries with which Western TNCs entered into partnership industrialisation are mainly in Asia, in some parts of Latin America (Brazil, Mexico and Chile) and in some parts of Eastern Europe (Turkey and Poland). The Southern countries that remain unindustrialised because Western TNCs are not prepared to enter into partnership industrialisation with them are mainly situated in Africa, Latin America, Eastern Europe and the middle East.

A major bifurcation has developed between those countries in the global South that became industrialised with Western support and those Southern countries that remained unindustrialised. In the former, a much higher economic growth rate has been attained over the past thirty years. The per capita income increased at such a rate in Asian countries that the unequal international distribution of per capita income between Asia and the West diminished. Those Southern countries that remained unindustrialised achieved much lower economic growth rates, while the unequal international distribution of per capita income between them and the West increased.

In those Southern countries that became industrialised with Western support, a relatively wealthy elite, consisting of 20 per cent to 30 per cent of the population, has emerged. These elite groups have become culturally Americanised and aspire to attain the high levels of consumerism maintained by Western countries. The wealthy elites act as intermediaries for, and collaborators with, the American-led global empire. Although these countries have succeeded in lifting some of their poorest people out of their misery, their domestic distribution of income has became considerably more *unequal* over the past thirty years – this is especially so in India and China. Such growing domestic inequality can undermine social stability. The American-led neoliberal empire succeeded in draining those Southern countries that became industrialised of a part of their wealth – but not as massively as it drains the Southern countries that remained unindustrialised. There, the political and economic elites that act as intermediaries or collaborators for the

American-led global empire are much smaller. These countries have also remained poor. In Africa, and in parts of Latin America, 70 per cent of the population still lives on less than $1 a day.

Over the past sixty years, the United States of America has built a new global world order that is – from an American point of view – a world of closed frontiers and open markets. The US is presently exercising its global power and its *imperialistic plundering* through this system of closed frontiers and open markets. The American-led empire was constructed with remarkable ingenuity. Its true nature, however, is diabolical. The US acknowledges the independence of all countries and – with the exception of a few 'rogue' states – also recognises the sovereignty of their governments. The frontiers of all countries are, therefore, closed, but the US has taken several steps – in some cases military steps – to ensure the openness of all their markets to infiltration and exploitation by 40 000 American TNCs and by 20 000 TNCs of other Western countries. The US has taken several unilateral steps to prescribe, directly and indirectly, certain 'global rules' that must be obeyed by the host governments when these TNCs infiltrate the open markets, and the global rules are regularly changed by the US to increase its 'imperial dividend'.[9]

In the years immediately after the Second World War, the Western countries with colonies in Asia granted independence to these colonies in what is known as the Asian decolonisation process, and in the twenty-five years after 1957 European countries with colonies in Africa entered what became known as the African decolonisation process. During the decolonisation of the Asian and the African countries, independence was granted to more than seventy erstwhile Western colonies. The understanding was that they became independent with sovereignty equal to that of Western countries but in most cases the newly independent countries were economically and organisationally (bureaucratically) not viable enough to exercise sovereign equivalence. With the emergence of the American-led neoliberal, global empire in the 1980s many of the newly independent countries in the South were in effect 'recolonised' – some to a lesser degree and others to a rather large degree – by the American-led neoliberal empire. Those Southern countries that became industrialised over the past thirty years have retained a reasonable part of their sovereignty. Their markets – with the exception of a few 'rogue' states – are quite easily penetrable by Western TNCs and IMIs. But those Southern countries that remained unindustrialised, and are rather highly indebted, lost a great deal of their nation-state sovereignty. In the case of these Southern countries the principle of 'sovereign equivalence' turned out to be fiction (see Burbank et al, 2010). It is easy for TNCs to move in and out of them as they please and to exploit them through what David Harvey (2003) has called 'accumulation by dispossession'. The criminalisation of the global economy by the emergence of the American-led empire has had devastating consequences for these Southern countries.

Joseph Stiglitz (2003) is of the opinion that those Southern countries that have been degraded to neocolonial satellites of the American-led neoliberal empire are either too powerless or lack the sovereignty to hold the large number of Western TNCs and IMIs accountable for the many malpractices these corporations committed regularly. Stiglitz blames the collapse of Enron in bankruptcy in 2001 on the deregulation of the corporate sector. He puts it as follows:

> [Enron's bankruptcy] has become emblematic for all that went wrong in the Roaring Nineties – corporate greed, accounting scandals, public influence mongering, banking scandals, deregulation, and the free market mantra, all wrapped together. [The] overseas activities [of American TNCs] too are an example of the darker side of United States globalisation, crony capitalism, and the misuse of United States corporate power abroad.

Stiglitz (2003) acknowledges that the rise of global *capitalism* in the early 1980s was not accompanied by the rise of global *democracy*. We are living in a global capitalist world but there is not a global democratic government to tame the excesses, the gross dysfunctionalities and the criminal acts of which global capitalism/corporatism are blatantly guilty. Stiglitz formulates the 'crisis' of global capitalism as follows:

> Unfortunately we have no world government, accountable to the people of every country, to oversee the globalization process ... Instead we have a system that might be called *global governance without global government*, one in which a few institutions – the World Bank, the IMF, the WTO – and a few players – the finance, commerce and trade ministries, closely linked to certain financial and commerce interests – dominate the scene, but in which many of those [in the Southern world] affected by their decisions are left almost voiceless [italics in the original].

The American ideologies of market fundamentalism, neoliberal globalism and consumerism

The rise of the American-led neoliberal empire and the ideological shift to the far right of the ideological spectrum was legitimised in terms of the ideologies of market fundamentalism and neoliberal globalism. These two ideologies were the American version of the British ideologies of free-market and *laissez-faire* capitalism in the nineteenth century. The British ideologues claimed that their free-market economy should be regarded as a self-regulating mechanism that operates in accordance with natural laws and would bring economic equilibrium to the British free-trade empire – and that the British government ought not to intervene in the economy. The ideologues of the American version of market fundamentalism and neoliberal globalism at the end of the twentieth century claimed that if all states in the world can 'roll back' their state intervention

31

and their economies can leave the organisation of the economy to their domestic markets and to global markets, the competition between TNCs and IMIs would create an equilibrium in the global market that would be to the advantage of all the people on the globe – if not immediately then in the course of time![10] Since the early 1980s, the corporate sector ideologues have propagated the ideologies of neoliberal globalism and market fundamentalism with evangelic zeal.[11]

According to these ideologues, all obstacles that restrict TNCs from operating globally *ought to be removed to enable the 'global market' – or in other words the American-led neoliberal capitalist system – to promote the well-being of all people in all countries in the world!*

The free-market ideology of *laissez-faire* capitalism propagated by the British economists at the end of the nineteenth century was highly unrealistic because it did not take the asymmetrical distribution of power and property within the British empire into account. The market fundamentalism and neoliberal globalism propagated by the American ideologues at the turn of the twenty-first century is even more unrealistic – and so much more pretentious – because they do not take the much greater asymmetrical distribution of power and property *between* countries in the global North and the global South into consideration. After the collapse of neoliberal globalism and market fundamentalism during the Great Recession of 2008-2012, the arrogance, the excessive self-assurance and the criminality with which the ideologues of neoliberal globalism and market fundamentalism were propagating their ideologies look rather ridiculous – if not plain silly.

With the knowledge of hindsight, we now know that the ideologues of market fundamentalism and neoliberal globalism did not have the well-being of all the inhabitants of the globe at heart, but that they were agents of an underhand 'imperial propaganda' to create the space and the opportunities for Western TNCs and IMIs to exploit large parts of the South for the benefit of the West, and especially the US. During the heyday of the American-led neoliberal empire (1983-2007) the international distribution of income between the West and Asia became slightly less unequal, but much more unequal between the West and the rest of the global South, while *domestic* income became – *in all countries of the world* – considerable more unequally distributed (see Maddison, 2007; Cornia, 2004).

When Western TNCs were empowered to enter into partnership industrialisation in some Southern countries in an attempt by the West to retain their control over Southern industrialisation, they did not foresee that consumer goods would be produced at such low unit labour costs in Southern countries that it would lead to considerable deindustrialisation in their own, Western, countries – deindustrialisation that led to growing unemployment and to growing inequalities in the domestic distribution of income in Western countries, especially in the US and in the UK.

Since the early 1980s, two powerful American trends have been at variance. On the one hand, consumerism ensures that the Americans (and the Americanised world) crave for more and even more consumables, while the advertising industry and mass media spur them on to remain unsatisfied and disgruntled. On the other hand, neoliberal globalisation and industrialisation in the global South have significantly reduced the income of the poorest 50 per cent of the population in the US. In an attempt to avoid a clash between these two trends, the US has instituted the following policies since the 1990s: consumers have been enticed with a policy of financialisation (or cheap money) to run up ever higher consumer debt. Second, vast quantities of cheaply manufactured consumables, financed by Eastern countries when they buy American bonds, are imported from Asia with the result that since 1980 the US has 'progressed' (or slipped back) from being the country with the biggest credit balance the world has ever seen to being the country with the highest debt level ever. Third, the US government (especially under President Obama) is trying to keep 'impoverished' consumers satisfied by providing extended social services (particularly health services) to the poorer Americans but meanwhile the Bush and Obama administrations have had to spend trillions to save the several big corporations – 'too big to fail' – from bankruptcy. While American *consumer* debt, *federal* debt and *national* debt are at record levels, the capitalist-orientated Republican Party flatly refuses to endorse higher taxes. The debt situation represents a serious crisis for the American-led neoliberal empire, for the country is trapped in an 'imperial crisis' by being too greedy and living at standards that are far too high, while its technological leadership and labour productivity have declined in relation to those of emerging industrial countries in the global South.

The financial crisis that occured in 2008 and the bankruptcy of many TNCs and IMIs, together with the trillions of dollars and euros that Western governments have had to spend to rescue corporations that were 'too large to fail', brought back an extremely important lesson for the Western world, namely that capitalist corporations cannot – and should not – be left unaccountable. No politico-economic system can be functional over the long-term if the democratic aspect of the dual politico-economic system is not powerful enough to hold private corporations accountable. While Western TNCs and IMIs have reigned supreme for about thirty years, many of the uncontrolled corporations and financial institutions were not only responsible for massive negative social and ecological externalities (especially in the global South), but also for an increased inclination towards corporate corruption and corporate criminality. After the bankruptcy of Enron in 2001 and the bankruptcies during the Great Recession since 2008, Stiglitz has been vindicated; he warned in 2003 that there are many more 'rotten apples' in the corporate basket than we suspected and that 'hidden theft had evidently been part of capitalism for a long time' (Stiglitz, 2003). In the Great Recession the American-led neoliberal capitalist global empire is in a serious crisis of survival because many corporations have become bankrupt or 'rotten apples', unable to be held accountable, while the financialisation of the global economy and the reckless speculation that facilitated it led to serious debt and moral crises in the US and in Europe. To complicate matters further, the ideology of consumerism that has been propagated so aggressively in the US since the 1920s and in Europe since the 1950s has seduced consumers into maintaining consumption levels that have inevitably led to excessive money creation (or easy money) and to excessive consumer debt.

The debt crisis in the US and in many European countries can have considerably negative implications for the global South – especially for the part which remained unindustrialised or became deindustrialised. The Western countries would in all probability use their imperial, financial and military powers to squeeze a larger imperial dividend from these Southern countries in a desperate attempt to solve their own debt problems. The question arises whether the political unrest that was experienced from 2011 in several Moslem countries in North Africa and the Middle East may have been instigated by turning the screws of the imperial grip on Southern countries by the American-led global empire and its sub-empires.

The ideologies of neoliberal globalism and market fundamentalism that were sold so triumphantly – and arrogantly – to South Africa by the Americans in the early 1990s now stand thoroughly discredited after the Great Recession and the American and European debt crises. The Americanisation of the South African politico-economic system during the transformation of 1994/ 96 was based on the wrong *ideological* premises, on the wrong *power structures*, and put South Africa on the wrong *development path*. The Americanisation of the South African politico-economic system was integrated into

35

the criminalised global structures and the criminalisation of the apartheid regime was replaced by the criminalisation of the system by American-led global capitalism.

Four Politico-Economic systems in place in South Africa 1652-1994

Mainstream economists (of the neoclassical school) are always concerned about the intervention of the political authorities into the allegedly self-regulatory functioning of a free-market or capitalist economic system. This attitude is pure 'economism' and not justifiable (see Teivo Teivainen, 2002). It betrays the ideological prejudices of that school of thought that regards capitalism as a sovereign system existing independently of the political realm, that capitalism operates automatically according to natural economic laws, and that the political authorities should not (and ought not to) interfere with the functioning of the capitalist market. Nothing can be further from the truth than this representation of capitalism by neoclassical economists.

Capitalism is not a sovereign and self-regulatory system, and it does not operate in accordance with natural economic laws. Capitalism is not a natural construct. It is a human construct and a man-made phenomenon. It is a project always in the making. A capitalist system cannot exist in a political or constitutional vacuum. Capitalism is always part of a dual *politico-economic* system in which the political authority, the state – irrespective of whether or not it has been elected democratically – represents the political side of the dual system, and capitalism the economic side.

Democratic capitalism, as a dual politico-economic system, only reached maturity after a long 'gestation' period. The democratic and the capitalist 'sides' of this politico-economic system are contradictory: *while democracy emphasises joint interests, equality and common loyalties, capitalism is based on self-seeking inequality and conflicting individual and group interests.* The legal system that protects both democracy and capitalism is based on the principle of equality before the law, but maintains inequalities in the distribution of property rights and of opportunities for the capitalist system. The 'logic' of capitalism – given the unequal freedoms and unequal rights upon which it is based – thus goes against the grain of the 'logic' of democracy.[12] Capitalism attempts to maximise efficiency and profit through merciless competition in a free market system in which the strong, skillful, and property owner wins, and the weaker and less cunning lose. It is the task of a democratically-elected government to attempt to reconcile the conflicting 'logics' of democracy and capitalism, but also to reconcile the 'power' with which democratic governments and capitalist institutions exert themselves. To emphasise the conflicting logics of democracy and capitalism is not to deny the complementary relationship between them. The strength and sustainability of the system of democratic capitalism depends on the mutual interdependence of democracy and capitalism.

Capitalism always needs a political authority (a state) to create the legal and regulatory framework and to enact the enabling conditions without which capitalism cannot function. The political authority (the state) can also not operate without the fiscal and financial support that the economic system supplies. As soon as a dual politico-economic system has been institutionalised, regular interaction between the political and economic sides takes place; the political side interferes with the economic side, and vice versa. Democracy and capitalism need one another in the sense that the power each exerts needs to be curtailed or 'counteracted' by the other to prevent the misuse of power by either of them. It is also important that neither of the two parts is too powerful in relation to the other. It is not advisable to study the history of political authorities (or states) in isolation from capitalism, or to study the history of capitalism in isolation from the history of the political authorities, for the interactions between capitalism and political authority should always receive the simultaneous attention that both deserve.

The Italian city-states of the fifteenth and sixteenth centuries were the cradle of capitalism. The modern nation-state system in Western Europe came into being with the Treaty of Westphalia of 1648, in which the sovereignty of Western European states and the European inter-state system were agreed upon and which also awarded nation-state status to the Netherlands. As soon as the Dutch nation-state came into being in 1648, it was taken over by the rich and powerful corporate elite in Amsterdam – and with that takeover capitalism was born in the Netherlands. Capitalism was born in England in 1688/89, when the mercantile elite and money-oriented landowners (the gentry) were powerful and rich enough to take over the English state during the Glorious Revolution (see Blaut, 2000). According to Fernand Braudel (1977), in both cases capitalism emerged triumphant when the business elites identified so closely with the state that they 'became' the state. Braudel (1977) puts it as follows:

> Capitalism only triumphs when it becomes identified with the State, *when it is the state*. In its first great phase, that of the Italian city-states of Venice, Genoa and Florence, power lay in the hands of the moneyed elite. In seventeenth-century Holland, the aristocracy of the Regents governed for the benefit and even according to the directive of the businessmen, merchants and money lenders. Likewise, in England the Glorious Revolution of 1688 marked the occasion of business similar to that in Holland [emphasis in the original].

Giovanni Arrighi (2007) agrees with Braudel's account:

> Add as many capitalists [or business corporations] as you like to a market economy, but unless the State has been subordinated to their class [the capitalist class] interest, the market economy

remains non-capitalist. Within China, large business organisations control extensive networks of commercial intermediaries... [but] capitalists remain a subordinate social group with no capacity to subject the general interest to their own class interest... [Consequently] China remains non-capitalist.

In the history of South Africa since 1652 a great variety of capitalist corporations have succeeded in 'identifying' themselves so triumphantly with successive political authorities (or with successive states) that they took over the states and (mis)used them to promote the narrow *class interest* of the capitalist/corporatist class to the detriment of society at large. This is, indeed, one of the great tragedies in the history of South Africa. There has never been a politico-economic system in place in South Africa in which the political side of the dual system was powerful enough (and representative enough) *to restrain the capitalist/corporatist side effectively enough or hold it accountable to ensure that the general well-being of society would be promoted.* Relatively small capitalist/corporatist elite groups were always powerful enough to promote their narrow corporate class interests and to neglect or to exploit the general interests of the majority.

We can identify four systemic periods in the history of South Africa from 1652 until 1994 in which capitalism/corporatism identified triumphantly with the state to attain control over the four respective politico-economic systems. In all four of these politico-economic systems, capitalist corporations always succeeded in manoeuvering themselves into such powerful positions that they were in the driving seat as far as political and economic decision-making was concerned. The four politico-economic systems that have been in place from 1652 to 1994 are:

(i) *The period of the VOC.* From 1652 until 1795 the 'government' at the Cape of Good Hope consisted of the representatives of the

Dutch East India Company (VOC). This 'government' was interested only in the profits of the VOC, and sorely neglected the interests of the white settlers, the Khoisan and the slaves.

(ii) *British colonialism during the long nineteenth century*. From 1795 until 1910 several British colonial authorities in Southern Africa represented the interests of the capitalist-driven British empire. These authorities were very concerned with the profitability of a variety of British corporations.

(iii) *The mineral energy complex (MEC) and the several South African governments during the first half of the twentieth century*. During the first half of the twentieth century the MEC – which consisted of a cluster of mining and energy industries – not only controlled South Africa economically, but exerted such great influence on the different governments from 1910 until 1948 that it was the effective governing body in South Africa.

(iv) *The MEC and the National Party (NP) government from 1948 until 1994*. The control of the economic side of the politico-economic system remained after 1948 – for all practical purposes – in the hands of the English establishment. Although the NP government promoted Afrikaner interests fairly forcefully in the 1950s, it realised almost from the start that it had to be very sensitive to the economic power of the MEC. From the mid-1960s there was growing cooperation between the emerging Afrikaner corporate sector and the established English business sector under the leadership of the MEC. In the 1980s the white business sector co-opted the NP in its desperate attempts to solve its accumulation crisis which was becoming increasingly more serious. As the accumulation crisis deepened, the effective government of South Africa shifted towards the MEC, which orchestrated the transformation process from 1986 onwards.

As the capitalist/corporatist side of all four politico-economic systems that were in place in South Africa from 1652 until 1994 was always much more powerful than the political side (or the state), it was never possible for the weak states to hold the capitalist formations accountable for their misdeeds or for the multiple negative externalities (both social and ecological externalities) for which they were responsible. Consequently, corruption and all kinds of highly doubtful and illegal business practices were always part and parcel of South Africa's political and economic history.

The Dutch East India Company (VOC) 1602-1799

The VOC was launched in 1602 as a chartered company. It was awarded a monopoly east of the Cape of Good Hope and west of the Strait of Magellan. It had the power to wage war, to construct fortresses and strongholds, and to enter into treaties and alliances in the vast zone comprising its monopoly. It was virtually a state within a state, a politico-economic system in which the political and the economic sides were rolled into one.

Over the whole period of its existence from 1602 until 1799 the VOC sent nearly a million sailors, soldiers and administrators on some 5 000 ships to its thirty trading posts in Asia. It was exceptionally profitable – especially during the first hundred years of its 200-year existence.[13] The VOC became notorious for the military violence it used against the Portuguese in the East and against Asian peoples to establish its fortified settlements. It also became notorious for its dishonourable business practices and for the large-scale corruption of which senior and junior officials were regularly guilty. The VOC has been described as the most corrupt corporation in the history of the world (see Charles Kindleberger, 1996).[14] But perhaps Enron should now be regarded as the most corrupt corporation in history.

The VOC established a refreshment station at the Cape of Good Hope in 1652 to minimise the large number of sailors who died from scurvy. The fortified provision station at the Cape developed into a colony, although this was not the intention of the VOC. But in spite of all the power and wealth at the disposal of the VOC, the company largely neglected its settlement in South Africa – the profitability of the capitalist corporation always enjoyed total preference above the interests of the white and black inhabitants at the Cape. The endemic corruption of the VOC was also evident in the ranks of the VOC administrators at the Cape as well as the colonial inhabitants of the Cape. In 1707, the Dutch governor at the Cape, Willem Adriaan van der Stel, was recalled by the VOC to Amsterdam for being guilty of widespread corruption and patronage.

For almost 200 years, the Boer Commando was the instrument of political power of the white Afrikaner pastoral farms. After every military campaign against indigenous population groups, the bounty was divided by the military leaders of the Commando among themselves in an arbitrary and corrupt way, with little concern for the economic plight of the ordinary impoverished Afrikaners, or subsistence farmers, of the Commando.

British colonialism in South Africa during the long nineteenth century 1795-1910

The East India Company (EIC) was established as a chartered company in 1600. In the first 150 years the EIC's operations in India were not nearly as successful as the VOC's operations in Indonesia. Its trading operations were restricted because it was obliged to pay homage to the powerful Mughal rulers in India but when the Mughal empire started to crumble in the first half of the eighteenth century the EIC started to act more aggressively against it. In 1756, the EIC deliberately violated its agreement with the Mughals by fortifying Calcutta against the French, who had occupied large parts of India. These actions precipitated the Battle of Plassey in 1757. After the battle, EIC officials went on the rampage and plundered large quantities of wealth from the Indians in a scandalous, immoral and corrupt manner. The EIC gained control of an Indian army that was financed by taxes from the Indian peasants. With this army, the EIC conquered the whole of India and other parts of Asia at no cost to the British taxpayer. From 1757 until 1947 India (and the Indian army) were extraordinarily important for the capitalist-driven British empire, especially in the forty years before the First World War and during the two world wars.

Britain captured the Cape of Good Hope from the Dutch in 1795 when it realised how important a gateway the Cape could be for the British empire in Asian countries and in Australasia. As the most advanced capitalist and industrialised country in the nineteenth century, the British colonial administration in Cape Town had the task of developing the Cape colony along capitalist lines to the advantage of the British settlers and corporations at the Cape. The economic interests of the Afrikaners were largely neglected, while large numbers of blacks were exploited by several repressive labour laws and by engagements in Frontier Wars.

When the Suez Canal was opened in 1869, the Cape lost its importance as a gateway to India but after diamonds were discovered in 1867, and gold in 1886, several British corporations started to extract the mineral wealth of the country. As Britain experienced growing balance of payment problems in the forty years before the First World War, and was also losing part of its gold reserves to Germany and the US, the British imperial government gave extraordinary support to the corporations operating the South African diamond and gold mines. A system of accumulation was established in South Africa that was characterised as a 'mineral energy complex' (MEC) where accumulation was and remains dominated by and dependent upon a cluster of industries, heavily promoted by the state around mining and energy (Fine et al, 1996). According to Fine et al, 'the Minerals-Energy Complex (MEC) lies at the core of the South African economy, not only by virtue of its weight in economic activity but also through its determining role throughout the rest of the economy ... The interests of the group producers [within the MEC] are coordinated through the century-old Chambers of Mines. Government policy towards the MEC is formulated through close coordination with the private sector.'

Sam Ashman et al (*Socialist Register*, 2011) described the importance of the mining industry and the MEC since the 1870s in South Africa's economic and political history as follows:

> The MEC has defined the course of capitalist development in South Africa since its minerals revolution of the 1870s, upon which extraction came to be based on the extreme exploitation of black labour achieved through a system of [African] migrant labour [introduced by several colonial governments on request of the MEC]. The discovery of precious metals and minerals produced a rapid inflow of 'English' or 'foreign' capital that quickly established control over the mining industry. Within two decades mining activities accounted for close to 60 per cent of exports from the region. The dominance of mining, and its need for large capital investment ... rapidly produced concentration in mine ownership in the hands of six finance houses or producer groups which consolidated their stranglehold over production, distribution and marketing through the Chamber of Mines [the public face of the MEC].

The mining industry became so important for the British empire, and the organisational pressure of the MEC and the Chamber of Mines became so compelling, that the British government was prepared to fight a costly and bloody 'gold war' against the two Boer Republics. During the Anglo-Boer War (1899-1902) the British government was also prepared to resort to crueller methods and used much more violence against the Afrikaner inhabitants of the two Boer Republics than other European empires were prepared to deploy against their European settlers in non-European countries.[15]

During the mineral revolutions, the British political authorities created conditions in South Africa that were extraordinarily advantageous for a small group of mining barons, enabling them to accumulate extensive wealth for themselves. The most successful of these mining barons was Cecil John Rhodes, who was not only utterly corrupt, but also most untrustworthy in his manifold illegal business and political wrangling to extend the geographical area of the British empire in Southern Africa. From 1890 until 1896, Rhodes was also prime minister of the Cape Colony. In this period state and business were represented by only one person: Cecil John Rhodes.

Political squabbling between the Afrikaners and English and the dominant role of the mineral energy complex during the first half of the twentieth century

In the decades after the Anglo-Boer War, all kinds of quarrels and hostilities arose between the two white settler groups in South Africa. This friction was experienced in the four colonies from 1902 until 1910 and it continued unabated after the four colonies were united in the Union of South Africa in 1910. From 1910 until 1924, the South African Party (SAP) of Generals Botha and Smuts governed South Africa on behalf of the MEC. The so-called 'Sappe' were a party of the English establishment with substantial support from Afrikaner elite groups. From 1924 until 1933 the Pact government of General Hertzog of the National Party and of Colonel Cresswell of the Labour Party governed South Africa: Hertzog supporters were the petty bourgeois Afrikaners and Cresswell supporters were the white labour class. In 1933 Hertzog and Smuts – who were for a long time sworn adversaries – agreed on a coalition government and then launched the United Party (or the 'fusion' government) from 1934 until 1939. When the Second World War erupted, Hertzog resigned and Smuts became prime minister again. His supporters were again the English establishment and elite groups of the

Afrikaners. From 1934 until 1939, South Africa was again governed on behalf of the MEC. Amid the political squabbling between the two white settler groups, the capitalist corporate sector – under the leadership of the MEC – played a rather prescriptive role in political and economic policies. Ben Fine et al (1996) describe the MEC as 'a system of accumulation'. They claim that 'while conglomerate ownership [in mining and energy] dominates the MEC core industries, control extends also to other sectors of the economy'. They continue: 'In the specific South African context, conglomerate power over the economy reinforced through simultaneous control of the financial sector is shown potentially to extend to all activities and sub-sectors within the mining, manufacturing and financial activities. This is possibly unique to South Africa'. Sam Ashman et al (*Social Register* 2011) gave the following description of the MECs:

> A system of accumulation develops through the historically contingent linkages which develop between different sections of capital - including finance – and their interaction with the state. The core industries [in mining and energy] influenced the development of other sectors and so indicated a specific form of industrial development. *In the case of South African MECs, then, it is not simply the weight played by the mining and energy sectors [that counts] but also their determining role throughout the rest of the economy. One merit of this approach is its capacity to conceive of the state and the market as integral parts of a capitalist whole* [my italics].

The MEC was responsible for the appointment of the South African Native Affairs (SANEC) commission in 1903 to determine why the Africans were not prepared to work on the gold mines. This commission's report led to the enactment of the Land Act in 1913 and to the institutionalisation of the highly exploitative migrant labour system for the gold mines. The MEC was also responsible for importing 64 000 Chinese mineworkers in 1903. The MEC was the driving force behind the process that led to the establishment of the Union of South Africa in 1910.

After General Smuts repressed the white mineworkers' strike of May 1907, he became the favourite politician of the MEC. The Chamber of Mines regularly wrote letters to Smuts to inform him what policy measures were necessary to enhance the profitability of the MEC. Smuts also repressed the strikes of 1913, 1914, 1922 and 1946 fairly ruthlessly. In 1922 he was even prepared to bomb the mineworkers in the hills around Johannesburg with military aircraft.

In 1920 the MEC decided to use fifteen black mineworkers (instead of the nine prescribed by the Mines and Works Act of 1911) for every white foreman in the gold mines to lower the cost of gold production. This decision sparked the Rand Revolt in 1922. The terms on which the Rand Revolt was settled forced Smuts to enact the Industrial Reconciliation Act (1924), which prescribed that nine Africans should be used for one white foreman on the mines. It was a huge – but unavoidable – defeat for the MEC. After this defeat the MEC used other methods to keep production costs as low as possible (as late as 1969 the wages of migrant workers on the mines were still below the 1896 level (see O'Meara, 1996)). The blame for the exploitation of African mineworkers by the ultra-repressive labour laws should not be placed on Afrikaner political parties, but should be put squarely on the shoulders of the English-oriented MEC. The Afrikaner political parties were concerned about discriminatory legislation to protect poor white Afrikaners, but it was the English-owned corporations which had influence over the repressive measures and the wages and living conditions of African labour.

The English-oriented governments of South Africa from 1910 until 1924, and again from 1933 until 1948, worked closely with the MEC and were responsible for comprehensive networks of patronage to the benefit of the English corporate sector. One of the most important 'favours' that was granted to the De Beers diamond company was the making of a criminal offence for private persons to possess uncut diamonds. It is quite remarkable that MEC corporations that held several monopolistic positions were always the ideologues for free-market capitalism. While De Beers maintained its monopoly in the cutting and selling of diamonds worldwide, it and the Anglo American Corporation launched and financed the Free Market Foundation in 1977, hypocrisy typical of the MEC.

South Africa did not devalue the South African pound when Britain abolished the Gold Standard and devalued sterling in September 1931. When South Africa devalued its money in December 1932, the price of gold increased by 45 per cent. When the Hertzog government threatened to tax away this 'gold bonanza', the Chamber of Mines pressurised Smuts into entering into a coalition with Hertzog to prevent him from doing this. During the negotiations between Hertzog and Smuts, they agreed that only 50 per cent of the bonanza would be taxed and that Smuts would support Hertzog in removing Africans – with entrenched franchise rights in the Cape Province – from the common voters' role. So this ugly and immoral horse trading between Hertzog and Smuts should ultimately be blamed on the MEC.

Legislation that the MEC did not succeed in preventing were the discriminatory measures enacted to protect Afrikaners against competition from, and contact with, blacks. The fact that Afrikaners had franchise rights and were strongly represented in parliament prevented the MEC from blocking these laws.[16]

Although the contribution of the mining industry to the South African economy has been enormous, its destructive impact on African society and its negative ecological externalities should not be underestimated. The migrant labour system destroyed the social and familial structures of tradition-oriented African societies. The security and health conditions in the gold mines were appalling.

Thousands died in mine accidents. Even greater numbers contracted tuberculosis and were sent back to the native reserves so that their families could look after them until they died. The negative ecological externalities resulting from the mining and energy industries were extremely severe: the most important of these are the poisoning of the subterranean water system in Gauteng and North West province. It is shocking that the mining industry (and especially the Anglo-American Corporation) is not prepared to take responsibility for clearing up the mess for which it was responsible.

Two negative legacies of the dominant position of the MEC should also be mentioned. First, the migrant labour system – which has been in place for sixty years – destroyed the 'native reserves' ecologically and, concomitantly, peasant farming. Second, the MEC's dominant position prevented attempts to diversify out of the core base of the MEC to create a viable industrial sector (see Ashman et al, 2011). Although considerable import-substituting industrialisation (ISI) was experienced during the Second World War and was also strongly supported by the NP government after 1948, South Africa has experienced a decline in its manufacturing since 1994. South Africa is today a developing country in the global South that is confronted with serious unemployment problems. It is important to realise that without an African peasantry and without a well-developed industrial sector it will be almost impossible to reduce unemployment to tolerable levels. The MEC has to be blamed for this state of affairs.

The NP government and the rapprochement between English and Afrikaner corporations under the leadership of the MEC 1948-1994

The Afrikaner establishment captured political power when the NP won the 1948 election on an anti-capitalist and pro-apartheid platform. The English establishment was dumbstruck by the NP victory.

O'Meara (1996) puts it as follows: 'Given the NP's overt intention to promote purely Afrikaner interest against the predominant economic power centres [of white English speakers] [the NP] accession to office struck pure terror in the hearts of most anglophile businessmen.' The NP victory was regarded as the death knell of the free enterprise system. At that stage the Afrikaners' share of the economy outside the agricultural and public sectors was less than 10 per cent.

The politico-economic system in place after 1948 was suddenly turned into an awkward one. The Afrikaner establishment that controlled the political side of the dual system was rather hostile towards the English establishment and the English establishment that controlled the economic side was in its turn hostile towards the Afrikaner establishment. The English-speakers were of the opinion that the NP government did not have the knowledge and capacity to govern the country. The distrustful relationship between the two establishment camps became even more hostile when the NP government enacted several interventionist measures and also additional discriminatory (or apartheid) measures, during its first five years in government, on behalf of the poor white Afrikaners. Attempts by the NP to remove the coloureds from the common voters roll in the Cape Province led to increased hostility between the Afrikaner and English establishments.

It did not take the NP government long, however, to discover the extraordinary economic power and influence of the MEC. Early in the 1950s a working relationship was established between Harry Oppenheimer (on behalf of the MEC) and NP cabinet members. Strangely enough, the NP interventionist and anti-capitalist measures of import control, protectionism and additional influx control measures to restrain the movement of Africans turned out to be conducive to a higher economic growth rate in the 1950s and 1960s. Dr Verwoerd's Native Laws Amendment Act (1952), which created the *'dompas'* system for African men and women led to a decline in African wages in urban areas. This legislation was not only to the advantage of the emerging Afrikaner corporate sector, but also to the advantage of the much bigger English-speaking corporate sector.

During the 1950s and early 1960s, the powerful English 'mining press' criticised the NP government's apartheid measures relentlessly at a time when the English business sector delighted in the apartheid labour legislation that enabled South Africa to attain an economic growth rate of almost 5 per cent.[17] The stabilisation of the black labour situation through the additional repressive and disciplinary measures that were enacted by the NP government attracted a large influx of foreign investment from countries such as Britain, Germany and the US during the 1950s and 1960s. Corporations from these countries increased their involvement in South Africa to benefit from the cheap black labour that was available. This influx of foreign investment made a considerable contribution towards the consolidation and perpetuation of the apartheid system for far longer than the forty years. In spite of virulent anti-capitalist rhetoric in some Afrikaner circles, South Africa in the 1960s again became a typically capitalist country in which the corporate sectors in Johannesburg and London were much more powerful than the political powers in Pretoria. Corporate power in Johannesburg was mainly concentrated in the hands of the MEC.

Ben Fine et al (1996) describe the influence of the MEC on the relations between English and Afrikaner corporations and on post-war industrial policy as follows:

> As a system of accumulation, the underlying trust of the MEC over the post-war period was the empowerment of Afrikaner capital, ultimately fostering the latter's successful interpenetration and coordination with English capital...[This approach] has had a profound impact on industrial policy from the 1950s, reducing it to three relative uncoordinate and even incoherent components: the creation of state corporations, mainly around the MEC; the application of

trade policy through tariff protection; and policies to promote industrial decentralisation and small businesses. This has led to policies which both supported the MEC's core sectors and precluded the adoption of other industrial policies of diversification away from heavy reliance on South Africa's resource but ...[consequently] the industrial policies that actually were pursued... followed a different path from that promoting industrialisation.

In 1964 Harry Oppenheimer took the initiative on behalf of the MEC to set up a working relationship with the Afrikaner corporate sector and with the NP in a 'partnership' relationship. Oppenheimer offered the Afrikaner business sector an attractive Afrikaner Economic Empowerment (AEE) deal. When one of the major Johannesburg mining houses, the General Mining and Finance Corporation, got into difficulties in 1964, Oppenheimer's Anglo-American Corporation took it over and offered it to Federale Mynbou, the mining subsidiary of Sanlam, which controlled Federale Volksbeleggings, at a fraction of its value. When this first AEE deal was struck, General Mining became an Afrikaner-controlled corporation.[18] Shortly after Sanlam's, Anglo-American created its own AEE company, Real, through its financial service subsidiary Southern Life.

Although the power of the NP government was very much restricted by the power of the MEC and foreign investments, the NP nonetheless used the restricted sovereignty at its disposal fairly energetically to install comprehensive networks of patronage for Afrikaner groups. I can mention the following: first, employment opportunities were created for Afrikaners by turning the English-oriented public and semi-public sectors into Afrikaner-oriented sectors within a decade. (It it not easy to decide whether the Afrikaner version of affirmative action in the 1950s or the African version since 1994 was the more destructive). The NP government used of the fact that both English and Afrikaans were official languages to get rid of those English-speakers in the public sector that could not speak Afrikaans. It took the NP government only ten years to turn the public and semi-public sectors into Afrikaner-controlled sectors. The Native Affairs Department (NAD) was very much enlarged, and Afrikaners with no experience in administration were appointed in it. The Afrikaner controlled NAD became notorious for the harshness with which it enforced the dompas system from the 1950s until the 1980s over Africans.

Second, the Afrikaner agricultural sector – which delivered the victory to the NP in 1948 – was heavily subsidised in the thirty years from 1948 until 1978. As a result of the sharp increase in government spending on defence and on African education after the Soweto unrest, the NP government could not maintain its high spending on the agricultural sector in the early 1980s. The scaling down of agricultural subsidies evoked sharp hostility against the NP from conservative (or *verkrampte*) farmers, especially in the maize triangle of the Transvaal and Orange Free State. This hostility led to the launch of the Conservative Party in 1981.

Third, the NP extended the public corporations such as Eskom, Iscor and the SABC, and established Sasol (through the Industrial Development Corporation), to create a greater number of employment opportunities for Afrikaner workers and training opportunities for aspirant Afrikaner entrepreneurs.

Afrikaner patronage underwent an important shift in the early 1960s. While it was originally targeted at the upliftment of poor Afrikaners, in the 1960s it focused on promoting the interests of the rich Afrikaner farmers and the larger Afrikaner corporations. After the NP succeeded with the rise to middle class of the Afrikaners in the early 1970s, the cult of riches became part of the *Weltanschauung* (world view) of, say, the top 20 per cent of Afrikaners. They aspired to become as rich and as inclined towards conspicuous consumption as the richer English-speakers. All the measures to promote the interests of the Afrikaners in the third quarter of the century led to more exploitative labour patterns as the *dompas* system was applied progressively more strictly by the Afrikaner bureaucrats. The bureaucratic red-tape connected with the *dompas* became so exhaustive that many Africans deliberately ignored it and became criminalised and even brutalised by the system. The per capita income of Africans as a percentage of the per capita income of the whites declined from 8,9 per cent in 1946 to 6,8 per cent in 1970 (see Terreblanche, 2002).

The situation in South Africa changed radically early in the 1970s. In 1973 an 'unlawful' strike by African trade unions took place in Durban. OPEC increased the price of oil rather sharply in 1973. In April 1974, General Spinola succeeded with his *coup d'état* in Lisbon and when Angola and Mozambique became independent in 1975 with governments supported by the Soviet Union, South Africa was, for the first time, directly exposed to communist infiltration. The Soweto unrest of 1976 signalled the formal commencement of the liberation struggle.

During the 1960s, the NP was of the opinion that the threat against the apartheid regime was internal and that it could be squashed by the police; consequently, South Africa was turned into a formidable police state by John Vorster during the 1960s. But the destabilising events from 1973 until 1976 convinced the NP that the threat against the apartheid regime was being organised abroad. The NP government increased its military spending quite drastically, from 2,2 per cent of GDP in 1972 to almost 10 per cent in 1989. The stagflation that was experienced by Western countries and South Africa in the early 1970s, was perpetuated in South Africa after the Soweto unrest. In South Africa's case the downturn became a *systemic downward spiral* that lasted at least until 1994. During this systemic downward spiral – that coincided with the liberation struggle – the annual growth rate declined to 1,7 per cent, while the real per capita income declined by 0,7 per cent annually.

Amid the deteriorating economic conditions in the 1970s and

1980s, the MEC and other corporations opted to replace the combative African labour force by capital-intensive investments and as a result the unemployment rate (according to the broad definition) increased from 20 per cent in 1970 to 36 per cent in 1995. The per household income of the poorest 60 per cent of Africans declined by almost 35 per cent from 1975 to 1996. The only group whose per household income increased during the period of creeping poverty was the top 20 per cent of Africans – by more than 35 per cent from 1975 to 1996 (see Terreblanche, 2002) – because during the two decades of stagflation the NP government pampered the emerging African elite in an attempt to convince them of the alleged merits of the apartheid system while the business sector pampered the emerging African elite in an attempt to convince them of the alleged merits of free-market capitalism. The more or less six million blacks whose per household income increased rather sharply became the core of the enriched black elite of today.

An important consequence of the worsening of the security and the economic position in the 1970s and 1980s led to closer partnership relations of the two white corporate sectors under the leadership of the MEC (see Van der Westhuizen, 2007). At the Carlton (1979) and the Good Hope (1981) conferences, a White Triple Alliance (WTA) was forged between the two white corporate sectors and the NP government. As the survival crisis of white-dominated South Africa deteriorated during the 1980s, the MEC acted increasingly as the leader of WTA, and in the local and the foreign crises of 1986 the MEC became the undisputable leader of the WTA. It is in this capacity that the MEC orchestrated the transformation process from 1986 onwards.

Sam Ashman et al (Socialist Register, 2011) describe how the MEC collaborated with the regime in the final years of apartheid to 'deliver' a transition advantageous to business:

Apartheid offered the most virulent and extreme form of racialised capitalism and, in its final years, had been based in its MEC upon an extraordinarily close *collaboration between the [apartheid] state and conglomerate capital*, prompting and ultimately delivering a transition [in South Africa] highly advantageous to [the MEC's] continuing and shifting imperative.

As the war against Swapo in Angola and against Frelimo in Mozambique intensified during the 1980s, the NP launched an ideological war against its foreign enemies. This ideological war was premised on the notion that South Africa was threatened by a 'total onslaught' that was organised, orchestrated and financed from Moscow and that South Africa needed a 'total strategy' to counteract it. In the 1980s the construction of this total strategy led to the securicratisation of South Africa. The South African corporate sector under the leadership of the MEC participated actively with the NP in implementing the total strategy and benefitted handsomely from the securicratisation of South Africa.

Events that weakened the power and prestige of the NP government in the 1970s led to the derailment of its comprehensive networks of patronage into open corruption. Although the Muldergate corruption scandal erupted only in 1978, there is little doubt that corruption was part and parcel of the NP policy arsenal from the outset in 1948. Nepotism in the allocation of licences and business contracts were the order of the day. Much of this allocation of special privileges was achieved through networks of the Afrikaner Broederbond. After the Muldergate scandal the PW Botha government used the budget of the Department of Defence to channel funds towards doubtful and corrupt projects.[19] One of the projects that was channelled through the books of the Department of Defence was the construction of Armscor. In the stagnant 1980s, Armscor was one of the few active concerns from which the MEC profited greatly. Another example other NP government's corruption was the huge amounts spent on decentralised industrial projects on the 'borders' of the homelands. This expenditure was notorious for the bribery that accompanied it. It is remarkable that South Africa's besieged position from 1986 – when the US Congress installed a comprehensive divestment policy against South Africa – motivated the majority of the English-speakers to vote for the NP to offset the large number of Afrikaners who supported the Conservative Party in the elections of 1987 and 1989.

During FW De Klerk's tenure of the presidency from 1989 until 1994, the government deficit increased from R91,2 billion to R237 billion (incurrent prices). We can regard this outrageous increase in the public debt as part of reckless white 'plundering' in the final years of white supremacy and, therefore, as another example of Afrikaner/white corruption. The question of whether the apartheid regime of 1948-1994 was more or less corrupt than the ANC government since 1994 is one that can unfortunately not be answered yet. The popular perception is that the ANC government is much more corrupt, but this cannot be confirmed; the problem is that parliament was the highest authority in the country until 1994 and this enabled all the white governments from 1910 until 1994 to 'hide' doubtful projects rather conveniently, whereas the ANC government is part of a constitutional democracy. But we have reason to be very sceptical about the functionality of all the institutions that have been installed on the basis of the Constitution to prevent dishonesty, corruption, illegal activities and the dysfunctional government over the past eighteen years.

The Transformation of South Africa's Politico-Economic System as orchestrated by the Mineral Energy Complex 1986-2012

The mineral energy complex enters the political arena openly from 1986 onwards

When the NP government declared the general state of emergency in June 1986, and when the American Congress enacted the Comprehensive Anti-Apartheid Act in October 1986, the South African business sector realised that their crisis of accumulation was very serious and became convinced that a transition to a political dispensation that would include the ANC had become inevitable. The business sector, however, was confronted with difficult impediments: first, how to convince the ANC to abandon its socialist orientation; second, how to prevent the ANC from becoming a populist goverment inclined towards massive redistribution spending; third, how to ensure that capitalist corporations would remain in a dominant position vis-à-vis the new political authority in the new politico-economic system; fourth, how to convince the NP (and especially the conservative wing of the Afrikaners) about the inevitability of a political settlement with the ANC; and, finally, how to interact with the black and militant trade union movement after Cosatu was launched in 1985.

At the end of the 1980s the MEC and other corporations in South Africa were aware of the neoliberal counter-revolution in the United States that granted TNCs the power, the freedom and the space to extend their (legal and illegal) operations worldwide. While American and European corporations were 'set free' and empowered in the 1980s to operate globally, the South African corporate sector was still 'closed in' and deprived of opportunities to solve its serious accumulation crisis through global projects. For the MEC and the rest of the business sector this was a highly frustrating state of affairs.

In the latter part of the 1980s the MEC succeeded in convincing the NP to accept the policies of privatisation and the dogma of neo-liberal globalism, and in 1990 the South African Chamber of Business published *Economic Options for South Africa*, which defended the alleged benefits of a free market economy. It claimed dogmatically that 'free enterprise systems – where [they] flourish – are the remedy for poverty and ensured economic growth'. In 1993 the NP published its Normative Economic Model (NEM) as its official economic framework for a democratic South Africa. The NEM was at the time heavily influenced by the MECs and the American ideology of neoliberal globalism.

In 1987 and 1988 the MEC decided that it had to play a more active and open political role to bring about the necessary transformation in South Africa. The MEC decided to authorise Dr Zach de Beer, executive director of the Anglo-American Corporation, to perform a political role on behalf of the MEC. In 1987 he expressed concern about the socialist orientation of the ANC and warned that the ANC 'may wish to throw out the baby of free enterprise with the bath-water of apartheid'. He also declared that it is part of the political task of the business sector 'to bring the benefits of the [free enterprise] system more and more within the reach of our black citizens' (quoted by *The Citizen*, 17 September 1987). In August 1988 the Consultative Business Movement (CBM) was launched with Zach de Beer as one of the initiators. The express purpose of the CBM was to challenge South African businesspeople to 'define the real nature of their own power, and to identify how they can best use this not inconsequential power to advance the society towards non-racial democracy' (see O'Meara, 1996).

In an interview with *Leadership* (Vol. 7, No. 3, 1988) Zach de Beer spelt out the reasons why the business sector decided to play a more active political role: 'Business felt [in 1986] its existence threatened by government's failure to maintain internal peace and tolerable external relations. Business was [in 1986] prepared to go to greater lengths than ever before in urging liberal change.'[20] In August 1988 the MEC, not satisfied with the performance of the PFP in the general election of May 1987, decided to replace Colin Eglin with Zach de Beer as leader of the Progressive Federal Party (PFP). De Beer immediately announced his determination to seek unity with Dennis Worrall's Independent Party (IP) and Wynand Malan's National Democratic Movement (NDM). I and several of my colleagues at the University of Stellenbosch became involved in the 'independent movements' of Worrall and Malan. After PW Botha's disastrous Rubicon speech on 15 August 1985 in Durban, about thirty Stellenbosch professors became very concerned about South Africa's financial situation vis-à-vis foreign countries. In October 1985 we decided to launch a new discussion group and called it Discussion Group 85. I became chairman of the Group. We compiled a memorandum on the crisis in South Africa, and in January 1986 we sent it to Chris Heunis, the minister of constitutional affairs. In the memorandum we stated, inter alia, that our impression was that all kinds of 'conceptual blockages' had crept into the thought processes of the leadership core of the NP and that these blockages prevented the government: first, from making a proper evaluation of the deteriorating situation in South Africa; and, second, from realising the unavoidability of negotiating with the ANC. We stated categorically that we regarded the ANC as a relevant actor in the dynamics of South African politics and that it had the ability to undermine any settlement with other black leaders.

Heunis, however, was not prepared to table our memorandum before the cabinet committee on constitutional matters or to invite us to testify before the committee. After an exchange of letters between our Group 85 and Heunis, it was arranged that the whole group of twenty-eight professors would have an interview with PW Botha at Tuynhuys on 20 February 1987. Every one of the six spokespersons of the Group told Botha that there was not a single moral or religious argument to justify apartheid and that it was an immoral system that should be abolished immediately. Botha was furious. The meeting ended in chaos. On 7 March 1987, the Group issued a declaration in which we requested the government to commit itself 'unambiguously to share power effectively with blacks'. We also declared that 'all South Africans must be represented in the central parliament of the country and on all other levels of decision making'. Members of the Group also decided to nominate Dr Esther Lategan as an independent candidate for the Stellenbosch constituency in the general election of 6 May 1987. During the election campaign the three 'independent' candidates, Malan (in Randburg), Worrall (in Helderberg) and Lategan (in Stellenbosch) drew a lot of attention and unexpected support.[21]

After I wrote an article in *Leadership* of April 1987 in which I stated that the NP has become a stumbling block *en route* to meaningful reform, and expressed my wish that it should fall to pieces, I became the favourite of the English business sector.[22] I was wined and dined, courtesy of Harry Oppenheimer, in Johannesburg and London. The Anglo-American Corporation sponsored me on several visits to anti-apartheid conferences in foreign countries. The six clandestine meetings in which I was involved with ANC leaders in Britain together with Willie Esterhuyse, Willem de Klerk and Marius Wiechers from October 1987 were financed by Consolidated Goldfields (Consgold). At these meetings we were treated as if we were celebrities. Shell organised and financed a large anti-apartheid conference of white businessmen, academics and prominent black leaders at White Plains near New York in September 1987. Zach de Beer played an important role at the conference in building bridges between members of the PFP and members of the 'independent' groups.

The initiative of De Beer to seek unity between the independent groups of Worrall and Malan led to the merger of the PFP and the independent groups when the Democratic Party (DP) was established on 8 April 1989. I became the economic advisor to the DP and a member of the executive. At the first meeting of the executive council, the decision was taken that the election of September 1989 would be fought on the principle of one person one vote. In the four weeks before the general election on 6 September 1989, the NP and the Naspers newspapers launched the most atrocious propaganda campaign against the DP, trying to discredit the Afrikaner academics involved in the DP with all kinds of suspicion-mongering.[23]

The mineral energy complex, secret negotiations and the Americanisation of the South African economy

The ideological shifts that took place in the ANC's economic views from 1990 until 1996 can only be described as breathtaking and even revolutionary. The ideological shifts from an explicitly socialist and redistributive approach towards embracing the American ideologies of neoliberal globalism and market fundamentalism were so radical that all kinds of 'unholinessess' must have taken place behind the scenes during those six years.[24] From 1990 Nelson Mandela and Harry Oppenheimer met regularly for lunch or dinner and from early in the 1990s the MEC met regularly with a leadership core of the ANC at Little Brenthurst, Oppenheimer's estate. When other corporate leaders joined the secret negotiations on the future of the economic policy of South Africa, the meetings were shifted to the Development Bank of Southern Africa, where the secret meetings took place during the night. During these meetings an elite compromise gradually emerged between the WTA (under the leadership of the MEC), a leadership core of the ANC, and American and British pressure groups. The secret negotiations reached a climax in November 1993. At that stage South Africa was being governed by the Transitional Executive Council (TEC) comprised of eight members of the NP government and eight members of the ANC leadership core. The TEC decided that South Africa needed a loan of $850 million from the International Monetary Fund (IMF) to help tide the country over balance of payments difficulties. Before the IMF granted the loan to South Africa it requested the TEC to sign a document about the economic policy of the future government. If the 'statement on economic policies' is read carefully, it becomes clear that it was the GEAR policy of 1996 in embryo form. The document committed the TEC to the ideologies of neoliberalism and market fundamentalism. The TEC reached agreement on a historic compromise in November 1993, the elite compromise, which is the foundation on which the new South Africa has been based since 1994 (see Terreblanche, 2002).

There can be little doubt that the secret negotiations between the MEC and a leadership core of the ANC were mainly responsible for the ideological 'somersault' of the ANC. It was, however, not the influence of the MEC alone. There was also pressure and persuasion from Western governments, and from international institutions such as the Bretton Woods Institutions (BWI) and global corporations. A large group of leading ANC figures received ideological training at American universities and international banks on the alleged merits of neoliberal globalism and market fundamentalism. In fact, we ought to feel rather sorry for the ANC because all the other participants in the secret negotiations – the local and foreign corporate sectors, the National Party, the American and British pressure groups – were ideologically committed to neoliberal globalism and market fundamentalism.

The strongest foreign pressure on the ANC, in all probability, came from American pressure groups. In the years after the Soviet Union imploded in 1991, an atmosphere of triumphalism reigned supreme in American political and economic circles. The attitude was overwhelmingly that the 'American economic model' has triumphed and that every country in the world could only survive and prosper if it adapted as quickly as possible, and as completely as possible, to the American model of anti-statism, deregulation, privatisation, fiscal austerity, market fundamentalism and free trade. Promises were made to the ANC that as soon as the new government had implemented the 'American neoliberal model', conditions would be created in South Africa that would be conducive to the large influx of foreign direct investment, higher growth rates, higher employment and a trickle-down effect to alleviate poverty. The role of the American pressure group was, however, not restricted to exaggerated promises, but also included subtle threats that the US had the ability (and the inclination) to disrupt the South African economy if the ANC should be recalcitrant and not prepared to cooperate.

The ANC's acceptance of the American neoliberal model reached a zenith when GEAR was adopted in June 1996. Ashman et al (*Socialist Register*, 2011) put it as follows:

The [ANC] Government's adoption of the non-negotiable Growth, Employment and Redistribution programme (GEAR) in 1996 signalled the crude resolution of any conflict over policy and the full embrace of neoliberalism. *GEAR emphasised fiscal austerity, deficit reduction and pegging taxation and expenditure as fixed proportions of GDP.* Through GEAR, the government's stated macroeconomic priorities became the management of inflation, the deregulation of financial markets, tariff reduction and trade liberalisation as well as limiting government expenditure. *The irony is that while the rationale for these policies was to attract direct foreign investments, their actual effect was to increase the outflow of domestic capital* [my italics].

With the adaption of GEAR the MEC, the ANC and the American pressure group succeeded in Americanising the South African economy. In biblical idiom, we have every reason to lament the fact that the ANC was deceived on such a massive scale by false prophets who led South Africa, not to the promised land, but into a desert in which the poorer part of the population was doomed to live permanently in a systemic condition of abject poverty. In 1994 nobody realised that it would take only fourteen years before the miraculous American neoliberal model would collapse spectacularly in the global recession of 2008-2012 and in the unsolvable and multiple debt crises of the US and Europe.

On 11 February 1990, the day of Nelson Mandela's release from prison, he made the following statement:

> The white monopoly of political power must be ended, and we need a fundamental restructuring of our political and economic systems to address the inequalities of apartheid and create a genuine democratic South Africa.

It is twenty-two years since Mandela envisaged his Great Agenda, but very little of his agenda has been realised. The new politico-economic system that was institutionalised during the negotiations turned out to be highly *dysfunctional*. Granted, the socio-economic legacy bequeathed by the apartheid regime to the ANC was in many aspects a bankrupt one. But one can see with the wisdom of hindsight that without doubt the opportunity to create a politico-economic system that could have addressed the deeply ingrained and deep-seated poverty problem was squandered when a neoliberal politico-economic system was institutionalised to serve the narrow interests of the old white elite and the emerging black elite, and when the enabling conditions of the new system were moulded in such a way that the imperial aspirations of the American-led neoliberal empire would be satisfied. While the capitalist/corporatist side of the new politico-economic sector has been extraordinarily powerful since 1994, the political side contained several constraints that deprived the ANC government of the capacity to execute governance with efficiency, effectiveness and compassion towards the impoverished majority.

The elite compromise that was reached at the secret negotiations was an agreement between a variety of local and foreign elite groups. The compromise that was ultimately agreed upon was one on behalf of the narrow class interests of each one of the participant elite groups, while the interests of the majority of South Africans, who were not represented in the secret negotiations, were terribly neglected. The elite compromise emphatically excluded the possibility of a comprehensive redistribution policy, which was regarded as unaffordable *after* preference was given to addressing the interests of the old white corporate elite and the emerging black elite, and *after* the conditionalities prescribed by the American-led neoliberal empire were accepted. The fact that taxation and expenditure as proportions of GDP were fixed by the elite compromise deprived the ANC government of the ability to implement a comprehensive redistributive policy.

The inequalities of apartheid to which Mandela referred in 1990 were indeed a deeply ingrained problem. From 1917 until 1980 the per capita income of Africans had always been less than 10 per cent of the per capita income of whites. The politico-economic system of white political dominance and racial capitalism, which had been in place for almost a hundred years, enriched and empowered the whites (and especially the white corporate sector) *undeservedly*, and impoverished and disempowered blacks *undeservedly*. In the early 1990s there was a growing consensus in certain white and black circles that the nature of the transformation should be such that the whites (and the white corporate sector) would have to make financial sacrifices over a long period of time to address the systemic injustices of white political dominance and racial capitalism.[25]

From February 1990 until early 1992, all the ANC policy documents emphasised the need for 'growth through redistribution'. But when a reworked economic document of the ANC entitled 'Ready to Govern' was published in May 1992, the phrase 'growth through redistribution' was conspicuously omitted. Since then the ANC has never again emphasised the need for a comprehensive redistribution policy. Why not? Simply because the ANC was already, in mid-1992, in thrall to the MEC and by the American pressure groups to embrace the American ideologies of neoliberal globalism and market fundamentalism. The ANC shift from a socialist or a social democratic approach towards a neoliberal approach happened when the ANC compiled the 'Ready to Govern' document. With the knowledge of hindsight it seems rather ironic that we can claim that the ANC was all but ready to govern in 1992. It is twenty years later. Although the ANC has been the government of South Africa for eighteen years we could allege that it is still not 'ready to govern'. It is, however, necessary to acknowledge that the legacy bequeathed by the NP government to the ANC in 1994 was bankrupt to such an extent that it was almost impossible for the ANC government to govern South Africa with the necessary sanity.

It was of the utmost importance for the MEC to negotiate a settlement in which the power relations between the two sides of the new politico-economic system would be such that the capitalist/ corporatist side would remain in the same dominant position as before 1994. Consequently, the local and global corporate sectors went out of their way to box in the leadership core of the ANC so thoroughly during the secret negotiations that it would not be possible for an ANC government to pursue socialist, populist or redistributive policies. The *quid pro quo* between the corporate sectors and the ANC leadership core was that lucrative opportunities would be created for the emerging ANC elite to join the white capitalist elite to become rich enough to maintain the same consumerist lifestyle as the white elite. The ANC leadership core was co-opted and bribed by black economic empowerment (BEE) deals, by empowering the ANC to allocate affirmative action (AA) and affirmative procurement (AP) contracts, and by giving the future ANC government full control over the budget on condition that the ANC would maintain fiscal austerity, deficit reduction and would keep taxation and expenditure as fixed proportions of GDP. The American pressure groups were quite adamant about the maintenance of fiscal austerity.

The interactions that took place between the Codesa negotiations on political issues at Kempton Park and the secret negotiations on economic issues (that mainly took place at the Development Bank) between leadership cores of the ANC, the MEC and American pressure groups, have not been revealed. That rather close interaction (or consultations) took place between the two versions of the negotiations is beyond dispute. One possible scenario is that the NP deliberately slowed down the Codesa negotiations to give the MEC enough time to box in the ANC with an elite compromise on economic issues. From February 1990 until September 1992, the NP negotiators (FW de Klerk, Gerrit Viljoen and Roelf Meyer) were strongly in favour of a 'statutorily entrenched minority [read: white] veto'. To put forward such a proposal was totally unrealistic. There was no reason to suspect that the ANC would accept such a proposal. But as long as that proposal was on the table, the NP negotiators at Codesa were playing for time. In September 1992, the MEC was satisfied that the ANC was boxed in sufficiently on economic issues in the secret negotiations, and so informed the NP on 26 September 1992 that it could accept the 'sunset' clauses.

69

The ideas about BEE and AA were important components of the elite compromise. It was decided at the secret negotiations that all black people – 91 per cent of the population – would be classified as 'previously disadvantaged individuals' (PDIs). Consequently, all BEE and AA transactions could thus be presented as 'redistributive' in nature and as part of the process of 'rectifying' the 'wrongdoings of apartheid'. Moeletsi Mbeki (2009) describes BEE and AA as follows:

> Most people in South Africa, in Africa, and in the rest of the world naively believed that BEE was an invention of South Africa's black nationalists, especially the ANC ... This [perception] could not be further from the truth. BEE was, in fact, invented by South Africa's [white] economic oligarchs, that handful of white business men and their families who controlled the commanding heights of the country's economy [the MEC] ... The object of BEE was to coopt leaders of the black resistance movement by literally buying them off with what looked like a transfer to them of massive assets at no cost. To the [capitalist] oligarchs, of course, these assets were small change .... Affirmative action and affirmative procurement, [which] started off as instruments created by the economic oligarchs to protect their assets, have metamorphosed. They have become both the core ideology of the black elite and, simultaneously the driving material and enrichment agenda which is to be achieved by maximising the proceeds of reparations that accrue to the political elite.

To classify the beneficiaries of BEE and AA as PDIs and to decide that there would not be a comprehensive redistributive policy for the impoverished majority – *who were the real victims of apartheid* – was a sham. From 1975 until 1996 the per household income of the top 20 per cent of Africans increased by more than 35 per cent and brought their per household income to R72 000 (in 1996 figures). In the same period the per household income of the poorest 40 per cent of Africans declined by more than 35 per cent, which brought their per household income down to R2 383 (see Terreblanche, 2002). The Africans who benefitted lucratively from BEE and AA since 1994 were, strictly speaking, no longer PDIs, while the impoverished majority have been shockingly neglected by the ANC by restricting the measures to 'rectify the wrongdoings of apartheid' mainly to BEE, affirmative action and affirmative procurement programmes for relative wealthy black individuals with contacts with the ANC's political elite. For the impoverished majority the 'injustices committed towards blacks' have been replaced by the 'injustices committed towards members of the black elite'.

The income gap between the top 20 per cent of Africans and the poorest 50 per cent has increased enormously since 1994 as a consequence of all kinds of lucrative privileges that were given to the ANC-orientated political and bureaucratic elite, and to the beneficiaries of BEE and AA contracts. As the power and privileges of black elitism were consolidated over the past eighteen years, the impoverished black majority was not only neglected, but actually betrayed by the ANC's leadership core. It is true that about 14 million people receive old age and child grants. Although these social grants are laudable, this cannot be regarded as redistribution, because they are granted to the recipients on humanitarian grounds. It is also true that basic municipal services and free water, electricity, schooling and health services have been made available to the poor. But as the infrastructure for these services has collapsed spectacularly and as the ability of the bureaucrats to deliver these services has declined conspicuously, the extension of these services does not seem to have brought a significant improvement in the standard of living of the many vulnerable people living in the many marginal areas in South Africa. In 2008, 17 per cent of all households (or approximately 10 million individuals) received no income from employment, remittance or social grants (see Leibrant et al, SALDRU, 2011).

71

It is conspicuously noticeable that all the elite groups that participated in the secret negotiations at Little Brenthurst and the Development Bank in the early 1990s have succeeded in gaining the 'great prize' to which each one of these groups aspired in the negotiations. For the MEC and the rest of the corporate sector the 'great prize' was to be exonerated of the huge apartheid debt that accumulated on their 'accounts' as they exploited black labour relentlessly over a period of a hundred years. On this issue the MEC outmanoeuvered the leadership core of the ANC by clever deal-making in the process of which the South African corporations were empowered to metamorphose themselves unjustifiably from ugly apartheid ducklings with a heavy apartheid debt on their shoulders into South African corporations exonerated of their apartheid debt. When the MEC and other corporations were given the *additional* privilege in 1997 of shifting their main listings to London and New York, and to become independent *transnational* corporations, the MEC succeeded in orchestrating a second unjustifiable metamorphosis.[26] With the two-stage metamorphosis the ugly apartheid ducklings were miraculously transformed into supposedly beautiful transnational swans, free to swim in all the global seas and out of reach of those South Africans who wanted them to pay a wealth tax. The only way to bring the transnational swans to account for their unpaid apartheid debt would be for class actions by the victims of these corporations to succeed in courts in London and New York, which is why it is of vital importance for the poor that the class actions in foreign courts should be successful.

The decisions that were taken during the transformation process in the early 1990s to exonerate the MEC and other corporations – which had enriched themselves extravagantly and undeservedly through systemically exploiting black labour and through systemically destroying large parts of South Africa ecologically – from all their apartheid and ecological guilt, while millions of the poor were left to rot in their abject poverty, were treacherous decisions that are going to haunt South Africa for generations to come.[27] As long as the white corporate sector remains untouched for the apartheid crimes they committed over a period of a hundred years, *the South African social problems – of poverty, unemployment and inequality – will remain unresolved and will become even more severe.[28]*

The 'great prize' for the ANC political elite at the secret negotiations was that they, and they alone, would be declared previously disadvantaged individuals (PDIs) who would qualify to become political representatives with lucrative salaries or would become the beneficiaries of BEE and AA contracts. The way in which the ANC leadership core has allotted political privileges to political insiders and the way in which BEE and AA contracts were allocated, turned out to be highly arbitrary and also the most controversial and most conceited part of the policies implemented by the ANC. While the ANC operated on the moral high ground during the struggle, since 1994 they have slipped into a sleazy underworld where corruption, nepotism and money squandering are the order of the day. We are reminded of Lord Acton's observation: 'Power corrupts and absolute power tends to corrupt absolutely'.

The 'great prize' to which the American pressure groups that participated at the secret negotiations aspired was to convince the ANC to accept the ideologies of neoliberal globalism and market fundamentalism, *so that South Africa could become a neocolonial satellite of the American-led neoliberal empire.* The implication is that the black and white elite groups are now the collaborators (or the convenient stooges) of the American-led neoliberal global empire, while the African poor and the unemployed are seemingly *permanently* and *systemically* excluded from participation in the global economy. The elite compromise made it possible for Western TNCs to play an important role in the South African economy. According to Mbeki (2009), 'the property rights protection enforced by the South African Constitution ... protects foreign investors. The sophistication of the South African economy and its extensive entanglement with the global economy means that foreign corporations have independent clout in South Africa in the sense that the economy cannot operate without international licences, patents, copyrights, and so on.'

We could maintain that the elite compromise was actually an 'elite conspiracy' that empowered and enriched all the influential groups that participated in these secret negotiations. The elite conspiracy excluded the impoverished majority and also the white civil service, which would be replaced – often undeservedly – when AA was driven too hard in the public and semi-public sectors. The elite conspiracy also excluded – in all probability – the manu-facturing industries and the trade union movement. The fact that Cosatu was responsible for compiling the Reconstruction and Development Programme (RDP), which was used as an election-eering document in the 1994 election and then discarded by the ANC government, is an indication that the trade unions were not part of the elite conspiracy.

It is rather alarming that South Africa is today a much poorer country from a *property* point of view than had been the case in 1994. Together with the massive outflow of long-term capital (especially when big corporations were granted the privilege of shifting their main listings to London and New York), we should also consider the one million (mainly white) South Africans who have emigrated since 1990. Many of them were highly educated, professional and experienced, and represent a huge loss of social and physical capital that was driven from South Africa when the ANC policy of affirmative action was driven in a myopic way and far too hard. Many of South Africa's corporations that became global cor-porations, the 'supposedly beautiful swans', operate fairly profitably in African, Asian and Latin American countries, and through their foreign activities South Africa has become a sub-empire of the American-led neoliberal empire. Although the South African internationalised corporations are making lucrative profits for their South African shareholders, their activities outside South Africa have in fact aggravated the problems of unemployment and poverty in South Africa quite considerably.

Ashman et al (2011) allege that government policy since 1994 has encouraged the outflow of long-term capital and encouraged the inflow of short-term capital. They put it as follows:

> High interest rates ... acted to impede domestic investment ... The high interest rates adopted as the government tightened monetary policy to reduce inflation have attracted an increase in short-term capital inflows into South Africa through the private financial sector ... The vast bulk of these inflows of capital have been channelled towards financial speculation and the extension of private credit to households ... *[In the meantime] the South African Central Bank ... has turned a blind eye towards the legal export of long-term capital that it has promoted and the illegal [export of long-term capital] that it had induced* [my italics].

The most harmful consequence of the Americanisation of the South African economy has been the *de-industrialisation* it has brought about through South Africa's obligation to implement a free-trade policy and to abolish all forms of tariff protection. This has had a devastating effect on many industries that operated for decades behind tariff walls. The clothing, textile and footwear industries were almost destroyed by the import of large qualities of cheap products from countries in the global South, especially China but while the free-trade policy was harmful for manufacturing, it was to the advantage of the MEC. These corporations, which are not labour intensive, are now in a position to import wage-goods cheaply for their relatively small labour forces. Mbeki (2009), describes the effects of the MEC's behaviour on deindustrialisation as follows:

> The outcome of the use of globalisation to provide cheap consumer goods for the working class in the MEC has resulted in the *destruction* of the non-MEC manufacturing sector. This explains why capitalists in that sector were excluded from the [secret negotiations]. It also explains the exclusion of organised labour. The destruction of the manufacturing sector is at the root of the growing impoverishment of South Africans, leading, as it does to increasing *structural unemployment.*

As was seen in Chapter Two before, the emergence of the American-led neoliberal empire in the early 1980s empowered Western TNCs to enter into 'partnership industrialisation' with corporations in Southern countries but the Western TNCs were only prepared to support industrialisation in Southern countries without high levels of indebtedness, with some ISI and EOI experience *and with a reasonably educated and disciplined workforce that made it possible to produce industrial products at unit labour cost that would be competitive in global markets.* This double-barrelled policy has led to a growing bifurcation between industrialising and non-industrialising Southern countries. The question arises whether South Africa should be classified – eighteen years after 1994 – as an industrialising or a non-industrialising Southern country.

In 1994 South Africa was in the grey area between industrialising and non-industrialising Southern countries but after the ANC government wholeheartedly embraced the American ideologies of neoliberal globalism and market fundamentalism, South Africa shifted into the category of *non-industrialising* Southern countries. The reasons for this shift are that South African labour became too expensive in global terms; that wages have consistently increased faster than productivity; that many black trade unions are too politicised and too successful in wage negotiations; that workers often acted in an undisciplined manner; that the AA contracts have increased the wages of AA beneficiaries far above the level of their productivity; and that the educational system, especially the township schools, was not delivering the productive labour South Africa desperately needed to be competitive in global markets.

The fact that South Africa has shifted into the category of non-industrialising Southern countries since 1994 has the devastating outcome that not only can South Africa not expect to attract enough foreign direct investment for industrial purposes, but it can also not attract modern foreign technology for industrial production. The relative *de-industrialisation* that South Africa has experienced since 1994 and the fact that South Africa is regarded by Western TNCs as an unattractive destination for partnership industrialisation both have gloomy implications for the situation of deteriorating poverty and growing unemployment.

The weaknesses of South Africa's constitutional democracy and the weaknesess of the ANC government

South Africa became a constitutional democracy in 1994/96. The South African democracy has all the trappings of constitutionalism. The Constitution prescribes universal franchise rights for all persons of eighteen years and older, and that elections must be held every five years on all three levels of government. Representation on the first and second levels of government is based on a system of proportional representation. The constitution makes a clear distinction between the legislative, the executive and the judicial authorities. A variety of legal institutions have been institutionalised to prescribe the relationship between the national, provincial and local spheres of government, while several checks and balances were also created to prevent the misuse of government power. In the legal system the Constitutional Court is the final arbiter on legal issues.

A democratic system is not only about its external trappings. A democratic system has two main functions. The first is to hold all institutions and all individuals, in all walks of life, accountable for the way in which they exercise their power and use their privileges. In this regard the elections that have to take place every five years are a crucial aspect of a constitutional democracy because they create opportunities for the electorate to hold the political parties (on all three levels of government) and their elected representatives accountable for the way they use or misuse their political power and fulfill their responsibilities. It is, however, not only politicians who must be held accountable. Through the network of public institutions, all persons and institutions in positions of power and privileges, in both the private and the public sectors, ought to be held accountable for their deeds and misdeeds.

The second function of a constitutional democracy is to furnish all citizens with a reasonably equal opportunity to influence government decision-making in a way that would enhance the *legitimacy* of the democratic process in the eyes of the citizenry as a whole.

If we asked, first, whether the South African system of constitutional democracy has succeeded in holding all institutions and all individuals in positions of power and privilege effectively accountable for the way in which they exercise their power and use their privileges; and, second, whether our constitutional democracy operates in a way that enhances the legitimacy of the system amongst the citizenry, then the answer to both questions cannot be anything other than an unequivocal 'no'.

I am going to identify eight weaknesses of South Africa's new system of constitutional democracy and of the ANC government. The first weakness is that the South African population is divided into different racial and ethnic population groups of very unequal size. The total population is composed of 80 per cent Africans, 9 per cent whites, 9 per cent coloureds and about 2 per cent Indians. With this kind of racial and ethnic inequality in the composition of the electorate, it is unavoidable that the African population group would play a dominant role in the democratic processes. This is not a healthy state of affairs – at least not over the long run. The fact that the Africans have been the main victims of colonial and apartheid exploitation and repression over a period of 350 years has nurtured a feeling of solidarity and togetherness, and the other population groups must acknowledge this feeling and display appreciation of the solidarity and togetherness among Africans. The danger exists, nonetheless, that Africans would be inclined to use their numbers and their ethnic solidarity to play too dominant a role, for too long a period, in South Africa's democratic system, making it impossible for our democratic system to fulfill its functions of accountability and integrity in a trustworthy way.

The ANC, with its explicit Africanist agenda, acts as the torchbearer of the African population group. In each of the first four elections since 1994 the ANC attained more than 60 per cent of the total votes cast. If it were to happen that the ANC succeeds in winning the next four elections, it would certainly not be conducive to the health and vitality of South Africa's democracy, as such an eventuality would be an indication that the solidarity among Africans is so strong that they cannot make an objective evaluation of the ANC government's positive and negative performances and would therefore not be capable of holding the ANC government and its office bearers effectively accountable for the way in which they govern or misgovern the country. Such an eventuality would also be an indication that South Africa's democracy does not operate in a way that enhances the legitimacy of the system in the eyes of the citizenry as a whole.

Many people have doubted whether a democracy can operate in a genuine democratic way when there are such great inequalities in the racial and ethnic composition of the electorate. South Africa's democratic system indeed runs the danger of what de Tocqueville has called the 'tyranny of the majority'.

A second weakness of South Africa's democratic system is that it is (after the elite compromise of 1993) too powerless to address the very unequal distribution of income between the 50 million inhabitants of the country, and also too powerless to address the very unequal distribution of income between the different racial and ethnic groups. These inequalities are indeed so large that they introduce almost unbearable tensions into the viability of our democratic system. A democratic system normally operates best in countries – such as the Scandinavian countries – with an ethnically homogeneous population and a relatively equal distribution of income. Given the huge inequalities in South Africa as a consequence of 350 years of discrimination and exploitation it is questionable whether our democratic system could *überhaupt* be viable and effective. An enlightened dictatorship may have been a better form of government in 1994 to address the serious inequalities in South Africa. But the problem is who would have decided on the successor to the enlightened dictator.

As far as the distribution of income of the total population is concerned, in 2008 the top 20 per cent (or 10 million individuals) received 74,7 per cent of total income, while the poorest 50 per cent (or 25 million individuals) received only 7,8 per cent. Further, 83 per cent of the whites (or 3,7 million individuals) were among the top 20 per cent of income receivers in 2008, while only 11 per cent of Africans (or 4,4 million individuals) were among the top 20 per cent of the population; 25 per cent of coloureds (or 1,1 million individuals) were among the top 20 per cent; and almost 60 per cent of Indians (or 740 000 individuals) were amongst the top

20 per cent (Leibrant et al SALDRU, 2010).[29] The really problematic aspect of South Africa's unequal distribution of income is that 95 per cent of Africans (or 23,7 million individuals) were amongst the poorest 50 per cent of the population, while 5 per cent of coloureds (or 1,3 million individuals) were amongst the poorest 50 per cent of the population. The fact that the Gini coefficient increased from 0,66 in 1992 to 0,70 in 2008 is an indication that income has become much more unequally distributed during the 'democratic' period (Leibrandt et al, SALDRU, September 2010).

The relationship between democracy and domestic inequality is a rather contentious topic, not only in developing countries, but also in the developed Western countries. When the power relations between the democratic and the capitalist sides of the politico-economic system of Western countries were based on a social democratic ideology (during the third quarter of the twentieth century) the democratic side was powerful enough to tame the capitalist/corporatist sector effectively enough to bring about an equalisation of the domestic distribution of income. But when the power relations between the democratic and capitalist sides of the politico-economic system of Western countries became based on a neoliberal ideology in the early 1980s (after Reagan's neoliberal counter-revolution), the democratic side was no longer powerful enough to tame the capitalist/corporatist side from enriching itself to the detriment of the majority. Consequently, the domestic distribution of income has become much more unequal since the early 1980s in all Western countries (Cornia, 2004).

The dual politico-economic system that came out of the elite compromise in the early 1990s, together with the embracing of neoliberal ideology, allotted such restricted powers to the political side of our dual system that it was not possible for the democratically elected ANC government to tame the powerful capitalist/corporatist side and to bring about an equalisation in our domestic distribution.

On the contrary, the BEE and the AA measures implemented by the ANC government led to the emergence of a black elite whose incomes increased considerably in relation to those of the whites and also in relation to those of the black majority. In 2008, 6,3 million of the 10 million individuals in the top 20 per cent of income earners were black. The percentage of blacks in the top 20 per cent increased and they became considerably richer.

In any country with the kinds of inequalities that exist in South Africa between the total population and between racial and ethnic groups it is of course not easy – if not, in fact, impossible – to implement an ideal distribution policy. In the early 1990s there was grave anxiety in white and in capitalist circles in South Africa that an ANC government would be inclined to be too populist and too redistributive in its approach. To allay their anxiety the MEC and the American pressure groups boxed in the power of the democratically elected ANC government quite considerably and made certain – when the elite compromise was agreed upon – that it would not be possible for the ANC government to implement a comprehensive redistribution policy. That was a great mistake because the ANC was empowered instead to implement several measures on behalf of black elite formation and to enhance white elite interests. The Constitution mentions several social and economic rights, such as the right of access to adequate housing, the right of access to health care services, sufficient food and water and social security. But as far as the realisation of all these social and economic rights is concerned, the Constitution stipulates that they can only be realised 'within [the government's] available resources'. It is sad that the realisation of these important social and economic rights has been made dependent on the judgment of technocratically-orientated ministers of finance.

A third weakness of South Africa's democratic system is that South Africa is a developing country of which a large part of the population is impoverished and 'underdeveloped' to such a degree that many are not capable of making a contemplative choice between the different political parties during a general election. We must appreciate the fact that many of the people in South Africa are so poor and so 'uneducated' that they never have the opportunity (or the luxury) to make choices between 'valuable goods'. They often have only one choice in life and that is how to stay alive. By being too poor to gain experience in choice-making, they do not know how to decide which one of the opposing parties in a general election is the most valuable one.[30] Yet poor people can participate actively in service delivery protests and to participate in these protests is part of the struggle for survival of impoverished people. But to use their votes during an election with the necessary reflection on the multiple issues at stake is another matter.[31] Of the poorest 25 million people in South Africa, almost 24 million are Africans. The fact that many do not have any experience in choosing between alternatives makes it likely that they would be inclined to vote for the ANC. A democratic election's result should not be determined by people who are too poor to cast a considered vote.

The fact that about 14 million people receive grants from the government is most laudable for without these grants their poverty would have been unbearable. But the fact that the grants are paid to them by the ANC government constrains the freedom of the recipients of the grants to vote and there have been allegations that, during elections, recipients of the social grants are threatened that the grants would be taken from them if they vote against the ANC.

A fourth weakness of South Africa's democracy is that representatives in South Africa's parliament and in the provincial councils are elected on a proportional basis. The system of proportional representation places extraordinary power in the hands of the National Executive Council (NEC) of the ANC. The NEC compiles the lists of candidates during elections and can redeploy members of parliament and provincial councils as they please between elections. The NEC plays a direction-giving role in the interpretation and implementation of the policies agreed upon at the ANC's national conferences. What is of special importance is that the NEC determines the networks of patronage and the nature of black elite formation in ANC circles. Given that many blacks were excluded for centuries from entrepreneurship and property accumulation, we should appreciate why networks of patronage and black elite formation should exist in ANC circles. It is important, however, that these networks of patronage and black elite formations should function as *transparently* as possible and that they should be *open to scrutiny* in the public arena. Unfortunately, it is not easy to establish the necessary transparency and accountability about what happens in the inner circles of the NEC. The process of black elite formation has derailed into a messy and corrupt affair that makes South Africa the laughing stock of the world. Over the past eighteen years a general perception has developed that matters such as patronage, black elite formation, tenderpreneurship and cadre deployment have taken place in highly doubtful ways, and that corruption and the wasting of public money are the order of the day in senior ANC circles. At the end of the 1980s the ANC – as a mass movement in the struggle – enjoyed a high level of moral legitimacy, both locally and in foreign countries, and so it is rather sad that the ANC as a political party and as government has squandered that moral legitimacy by acquiring a reputation of immoral deal-making, of money grabbing, of plundering the states coffers, of careerism, of greediness and of conspicuous consumption – and the fact that all these misdeeds occur in elite circles while 25 million black people live in abject poverty is mind-boggling.

The organisational power that has been concentrated in the hands of the NEC in the system of proportional representation also has another negative implication. It motivated the delegates at the ANC National Conference to turn the conference into 'battlefields' by voting for the leaders of different ANC factions in the anticipation that their specific faction will be elected. As long as the ANC remains the ruling party and as long as so much power is vested in the hands of the NEC to allocate patronage, the curse of factionalism will continue to haunt the ANC. This strong tendency towards factionalism has the potential to tear the ANC apart into irreconcilable groupings.

A last negative implication of the system of proportional representation is that it is inclined to stifle intellectual debate in the ANC and in other political parties and thus degrade the importance of representative bodies. Representatives who ask controversial questions and are inclined to give diverging interpretations of the policies of their party can be easily redeployed. From a genuinely democratic point of view this is a very unfortunate state of affairs. The system of proportional representation is inclined to paralyse parliament – and there are in fact indications that this has already happened among all the parties and in all representative bodies since 1994.

A fifth and rather serious weakness of our new democratic system is that there are not enough watchdog organisations in the private and public sectors to hold individuals and institutions in position of power and privilege accountable during the five-year periods between elections. Nef and Reiter (2009) allege that 'free elections are not enough to define democracy; and participation, social justice, equity, government responsiveness and transparency have necessarily to be taken into account'. It is against this background that all democratic countries need a large number of effective watchdog organisations in both the private and the public sectors that can scrutinise the behaviour of institutions and individuals. Some of the official watchdog organisations that were established in terms of the Constitution have been abolished or weakened by the ANC government. The Scorpions were abolished and replaced with the Hawks, but the Constitutional Court found that the Hawks do not have the power they need.

Civil society organisations played an extraordinarily important role during the liberation struggle against apartheid. While the ANC prepared itself to take over political power in the early 1990s, many civil society organisations were either abolished or deprived of the highly politicised roles they had played during the struggle years.[32] Fortunately, some strong civil society groups such as the Treatment Action Campaign (TAC) succeeded in influencing government policy on the HIV/AIDS pandemic. It is a pity that South Africa does not have many more civil society groups as strong, as well organised and as militant as the TAC to pressurise the government to be more attentive to poverty, social justice, equity and transparency – but as the government remains a captive of corporate dominance and globalism, and as the larger NGOs become increasingly involved in service delivery, promising signs are fortunately noticeable of new civil society groups emerging from the ranks of community-based organisations. These organisations are responding to the basic needs and the justifiable grievances of the impoverished majority although they are unfortunately not numerous enough and also not strong and aggressive enough to restore order, discipline and accountability in South Africa's rather chaotic democratic system.

The media have played an indispensable role since 1994 in disclosing government scandals and corruption. The danger exists, however, that the Protection of Information Bill (or the 'Secrecy Bill') may deprive the media of the most valuable role it has played to uncover many of the malpractices and excesses of the ANC government. The questions that were raised by President Zuma and by Gwede Mantashe, secretary general of the ANC, about the courts becoming the new opposition to the ruling party is a matter of great concern.

Both the 'Secrecy Bill' and the questions about the role of the courts are indications of paranoia in ANC circles about its own vulnerability and its own ineptness in governing the country in a transparent and democratic manner.

A sixth weakness of our new democracy is that the elite compromise has established such a close partnership between the ANC government and the corporate sector that it is often not possible to draw a clear line between the public and the private sectors. We should remember that the elite compromise was not a single isolated event. It created the framework for ongoing interactions between the ANC government and the corporate sector on matters concerning BEE and AA contracts. What we have experienced since 1994 is a continuation of the excessively close interaction that prevailed for the best part of a century between the MEC and the successive (white) governments. As the MEC was almost uninterruptedly in cahoots with white governments before 1994, there are indications that it and other corporations are again too closely in cahoots with the ANC government. When the dividing line between the public and the private sectors becomes blurred, as has happened in South Africa since 1994, the danger of all kinds of doubtful and secret business deals between the public and private sectors becomes a real possibility. We should not be surprised to find that many dubious deals that cannot be scrutinised by the normal processes of democratic oversight have already derailed into large-scale corruption over the past eighteen years.

What is quite remarkable about the 'partnership relation' between the ANC government and the corporate sector is that the latter is conspicuously silent about the many malpractices of which the ANC government is guilty. In 1988 the MEC was prepared to play a more active and open political role when apartheid was denounced worldwide as an immoral system. Why is the corporate sector at present not prepared to play a similarly open *political* role to

87

denounce the immorality and the illegality of which the ANC is now guilty? Is the corporate sector now experiencing an accumulation boom in contrast with the accumulation crisis that was experienced in 1988? Or has the ANC government become so self-centered and self-assured that it is not prepared to take reprimands from its 'corporate partners'?

The white corporate sector should realise that it cannot be exonerated from all the bungling associated with BEE and AA contracts. Such bungling has indeed become part of the business culture for which the corporate (or business) sector has to take shared responsibility. It would not be an overstatement to claim that, from an organisational and a moral point of view, the South African dual politico-economic system is in a very unhealthy state. Although the CEOs with their 'globally' inflated salaries would not be prepared to acknowledge it, they have a huge responsibility to clean up the mess into which South Africa has descended after corporate capitalism was the 'winner' and the ANC the 'loser' in the contest that took place between them in the mid-1990s. The white corporate sector should realise that the present crisis in South Africa is, like the Great Recession in the US, not only an economic crisis, but also a serious *moral and legal* crisis.

The seventh and very serious weakness is that the ANC government is powerless because its sovereignty is too constrained by the triple capitalist formations with which it is confronted: namely the successor of the white apartheid capitalist formation (mainly the MEC), the new BEE capitalist formation, and the global capitalist formation; and the close integration of the triple capitalist formations with their joint embracing of financialism and the American ideologies of neoliberalism and market fundamentalism. South Africa's position as a neocolonial satellite of the American-led neoliberal empire since 1994 has been, over the past eighteen years, conducive to reasonable economic growth (and for an increase of the economy's tax capacity), but not conducive to job creation and poverty alleviation. It is sad that the democratically elected government in South Africa is not sovereign enough to decide on its own what its policy priorities ought to be. Our democratic government could not give a higher priority to job creation and poverty alleviation – even if civil society organisations were to succeed in convincing the government *that it would be the right thing to do*. If the ANC government were to implement the needed redistributive measures, the danger exists that the credit rating agency would degrade South Africa's credit status.

The final weakness of the ANC government is that it seems as if the government has anything but a clear idea about what constitutes the *general interest or the general wellbeing* of the nation's 50 million people. This is not as it ought to be in a *genuine* democracy. It seems as if the ANC government also has no clear idea of the proper trade-off it has to make between the short-term interests of strong pressure groups and the long-term interests of the nation. It seems as if the government has also no clear idea of the importance of a fair trade-off between the interests of the 10 million rich people and the interests of the 25 million poor (see Arthur Okun, 1982, *Equality and Efficiency – The Big Trade-off*). Without a clear idea about the importance of this trade-off, the ANC is easily taken in tow by small pressure groups that only have their own narrow short-term interests at heart. It seems as if the ANC government has also no clear idea of what it takes to rule the country with *good governance*, with *transparency*, with *good judgement* and with *fairness* to all.

The ANC government's inclination towards short-termism over the greatest part of the past eighteen years is demonstrated by the government neglect of infrastructural investment until 2006. According to the Development Bank's *Infrastructure Barometer* (2008), public sector investment in infrastructure increased from about 5 per cent of GDP in 1960 to 8,1 per cent in 1976 and then declined to 2,6 per cent in 1994. This decline coincided with the period of the struggle and the period of stagflation when the NP government was obsessed with countering the alleged total on-slaught. In the first twelve years of ANC governments (1994-2006) infrastructural investment in the public sector remained on a level below 3 per cent of GDP. During this period the ANC government apparently accepted literally the neoliberal slogan of 'rolling back the state'.

The huge increase in infrastructure investment that was announced in the March 2012 budget is long overdue. The question remains, however, whether it is going to be spent on badly needed infra-structural projects, for one gets the impression that it is going to be spent on infrastructural projects that would facilitate the export of minerals to BRIC countries. Is this the sacrifice South Africa had to make to justify the S at the end of BRICS? Jim O'Neil (*The Sunday Times*, 1 April 2012) alleges that 'South Africa's inclusion [in BRICS] seems a bit hard to justify, given it is a much smaller economy than the other four. South Africa in 2011 surpassed $400 billion in terms of GDP, but this is about one quarter of both India and Russia, one-fifth of Brazil's and just one eighteenth of China.' Jim O'Neil (who ten years ago invented the acromyn BRIC), also emphasises the fact that the GDP of countries such as Indonesia, Korea, Mexico and Turkey are bigger than that of South Africa and that their growth rates as developing countries are also higher than that of South Africa. It seems as if South Africa's membership of BRICS may not be to our advantage. The intention of the BRIC countries may be to plunder South Africa's minerals.

chapter five

Affirmative Action and the Rapid Africanisation of the Bureaucracy

The American legal philosopher Drucilla Cornell writes a chapter in her book *Symbolic Forms for a New Humanity* (2010) on what she regards as the two main themes of *A History of Inequality*: 'unfree black labour' and how its story is related to 'shifts in political, economic and ideological power'.

In *Inequality* (2002) I distinguish between eight different patterns of 'unfree black labour': slavery, *'inboekelingskap'*, indentureship, several Master and Servants Acts, migrant labour systems, influx control or the *dompas* system, labour discrimination, and, ultimately the growing unemployment problem that has been perpetuated in the post-apartheid period. Almost half of black people are unemployed. Many of them do not have any prospect of occupying a permanent job in their lifetime.

Cornell et al (2010) make the following comments on what I have written about 'unfree black labour':

Terreblanche explicitly states that he is narrating history from a particular point of view, telling the history of South Africa from the standpoint of unfree black labour. The task for Terreblanche has been to 'explore South Africa's modern history mainly from the perspective of unequal power relations and unfree labour patterns'. Such an investigation traverses many intellectual paths, bringing to life 'the histories of power domination (political, economic and ideological) and land deprivation' to help unfold the 'drama of unfree black labour over the past 350 years'... [But according to Terreblanche] there has not been in South Africa the desperately needed change of power [since 1994] that would change the *nature* of power itself. In other words, although blacks now hold political power, they have succumbed to the dominant relations of *neoliberal capitalism* that were passed on to them by the preceding government and they have also become ideological props in defence of such neoliberal capitalism.

Cornell (2010) unpacks in great detail the philosophical meaning of 'unfree black labour':

> The 'unfree' in the term unfree black labour requires us to meaning-fully known freedom, which can be gleaned from the capabilities development work of Amartya Sen ... The 'black' in unfree black labour is a matter of understanding black consciousness as the way of life that would break the shackles of racial bondage imposed by the racist state in the sense meant by Steve Biko ... The 'labour' in unfree black labour demands that we return to Marx in order to understand the crippling effect of super exploitation.

After Cornell (2010) has discussed the failure of the ANC to transform power relations deeply enough in South Africa, she concludes that the history of South Africa 'can be read as a history of wreckage; a wreckage that forms the foundation to a main tower of so-called progress atop the graves of those who died by the hand of radicalised capitalists. Yet, with the idea of *black unfree labour* as a symbolic form, one that can be read through history with a telos, we are always pointed towards the reflective, regulative inverse that emerges: *free human beings*'.

After 350 years of 'unfree black labour' the labour situation that confronted the ANC government in 1994 was a serious and an extremely complicated problem. From 1970 until 1995 unemployment increased from 1,9 million individuals to 4,8 million individuals, or from 20 per cent to 36 per cent of the labour supply. The education and skill levels of African labour in particular were shockingly low because for every R100 spent on the education of white children in 1976 only R6 was spent on African children. Until 1975 the per capita social spending (including spending on education) on Africans was less than 12 per cent of the amount spent on whites. As recently as 1982, total spending on African education was less than half the amount spent on white education, although the African population was more than 4,5 times larger than the white population.

Repressive and discriminary measures were applied to black people in South Africa for 350 years. Most of the work done by blacks was unskilled and semi-skilled work. Sadie (1991) classified the labour force in 1985 in four categories. The first is the executive category (entrepreneurs, managers and directors); the second category comprises highly-skilled workers; the third category consists of lesser-skilled worker and the fourth category of unskilled workers. In 1985, only 0,1 per cent of Africans were working in the executive category, 5 per cent in the highly-skilled category, 30 per cent in the lesser-skilled category and 65 per cent in the unskilled category. The whites' employment pattern was, in 1985, almost a reverse image: 13 per cent of whites were employed in the executive category, 37 per cent in the highly-skilled category, 50 per cent in the lesser-skilled category and only 1,2 per cent in the unskilled category. It was therefore necessary to 'rectify' this situation with affirmative action. (The Afrikaans words for affirmative action are *'regstellende optrede'* – a better description of the policy that was so badly needed in 1994.)

The ANC was, in 1994, confronted with serious problems at the top and the bottom of the black labour pyramid. At the top of the pyramid, the representation of black people in senior or executive positions was very small while at the bottom the level of unemployment was very large – and growing.

Affirmative Action (AA) can be defined as corrective measures to ensure representation in the workforce of all races, of women and of people with disabilities. *The Employment Equity Act 55 of 1998* (EEA) defined AA as 'measures designed to ensure that *suitably qualified* people from designated groups have equal employment opportunities and are equitably represented in all occupational categories and levels in the workforce of a designated employer'. In a White Paper in the *Government Gazette*, Vol. 394, No 18800 (April 1998), AA is defined 'as corrective steps which must be taken in order that those who have been historically disadvantaged by unfair discrimination are able to derive full benefit from equitable employment environments'.

Amano Edigheji (2007) gives the following broader motivation of AA:

> The introduction of affirmative action (and employment equity in the private sector) was against the background of apartheid labour market policies that restricted access to skilled work for blacks, people with disabilities and women. This exclusion was exacerbated by inadequate education and training as well as limited employment opportunities, especially for blacks in the public sector. Another reason for the introduction of affirmative action was the democratic government's inheritance of a state that was not an effective and efficient instrument for 'delivering equitable services to all citizens and of driving the country's economic and social development'. This, the White Paper argues, was because of 'ineffectiveness, unfair discrimination and division on the basis of race and gender, and which virtually excluded people with disabilities'. This eroded the legitimacy and credibility of the public service in the eyes of most South Africans.

The EEA recognises black people, women of all races, and people with disabilities as the potential beneficiaries of affirmative action in the workplace. According to Ockert Dupper (2008) 'black' is intended to represent the designated group encompassing all those previously classified as 'African', 'coloured' and 'Indian', reproducing what are in fact the same racial categories and divisions that underpinned apartheid. Dupper is, however, of the opinion that the actual implementation favours 'race' over 'gender' and 'disability' and 'African' over 'coloured' and 'Indian'. According to Dupper 'this should not come as a surprise, because as recently as 2005 the ANC reconfirmed that the national question in South Africa is about the liberation of the African majority'. The preference that is given to 'African' above 'coloured' in the implementation of AA has lately become a tricky party political matter especially in the Western Cape. In the Commission for Employment Equity (CEE) 2011 annual report it is acknowledged that 'the representation of coloureds, women and people of disabilities still lags behind at most levels when measured against the economically active population'.

In terms of the EEA, candidates will have to meet two criteria before being considered for appointment or promotion under the employment equity plan. The first is membership of the designated groups; the second that they are 'suitably qualified'. Ockert Dupper (2008) indicates that the Constitution states that when decisions are taken about 'suitably qualified', the equality (or representivity) objective and the efficient objective ought to be taken into account. These two objectives need not necessarily be in conflict, but when when they are the trade-off between the imperatives of equity (or representivity) and efficiency should be a *rational* one. According to Dupper, 'the efficiency considerations in the private sector are largely self-enforcing with financial incentives compelling employers to define "merit" in a manner that advances their own interest'. The corporate sector in South Africa is in a rather strong position vis-à-vis the ANC government. It is also financially strong, and able to recruit designated candidates from the public sector. Jeremy Cronin (2005) described this trend as:

> ... the present trajectory of BEE policies is gravely undermining the capacity and coherence of the new state cadre. BEE targets

and scorecards imposed on the private sector now require very significant numbers of new senior black managers. A large number of these appointments have (and will increasingly) come from the new cadre in the state. The public sector has recruited tens of thousands of young black graduates, who have begun to acquire public sector managerial and sector-specific experience. However, there are extremely high levels of turnover among this cadre. There is much upwardly-mobile job-hopping within the public sector, but increasingly this cadre is being poached wholesale by the private sector, and our own policies are encouraging this.

The CEE annual report stated that in spite of the progress attained by employment equity over the years, whites still dominate the three uppermost occupational levels (top management, senior management and professionally qualified persons): 'Notwithstanding the fact that blacks account for approximately 86 per cent of employees contained in reports received, they only account for 16,9 per cent of the top management level and 35,9 per cent of the senior management level ... From the eleven sectors identified ... the community, social and personnel service sectors appears to be consistently performing well across nearly all levels, which could be attributed to the numbers of state employers and employees in this sector.'

The question arises whether affirmative action has not been driven too hard in the public sector. According to Moeletsi Mbeki, the ANC's AA policy 'promotes incompetence and corruption in the public sector by using ruling party allegiance and connections as the criteria for entry and promotion in the public service, instead of having tough public service examination'. As the NP turned the public sector in the 1950s from an English-orientated sector within 10 years into an Afrikaner-orientated sector, it seems as if the ANC government has succeeded to turn large parts of mainly the second and third levels of the bureaucracy into an African-orientated sector.

According to the CEE, many heart-warming stories exist of successful promotions, effective mentoring and training and lucrative BEE business partnerships. Statistics show that South Africa's labour market is slowly transforming as more Africans become profession-ally qualified (now 31 per cent of all economically active Africans, up from 20,2 per cent in 2006) or skilled (now 51 per cent of all economically active Africans, up from 39,2 per cent in 2006). But transformation, so far, has not been broad based.

The percentage of black people 'suitably qualified' for high level employment was much smaller in 1994 than that of Afrikaners in the 1950s and the totally inadequate education for blacks in apartheid years is to blame. The educated and skilled black people in the relatively small pool were employed from 1994 in positions in the private sector, in the black political sector and in the bureaucracy on the first level of government. When that pool of educated and skilled black people became depleted, the ANC government con-tinued to appoint and to promote black people – especially on the second and third levels of the bureaucracy – in spite of the fact that many of them were not 'suitably qualified' or could not pass tough public service examinations. The implications of this strategy is that large scale cadre deployment, motivated by party political considerations, is taking place on the second and third levels of the bureaucracy. In these appointments, the objective of equality (or representativeness) are taken into account, while the objective of efficiency is discarded. The alarming decline in the efficiency with which the second and third levels of the bureaucracy deliver public services has a negative impact on the population, but mainly on the impoverished majority – and especially on those living in in-formal settlements. The trade-off between the cadre deployment of unsuitably qualified persons and the entrenchment of black poverty is a very irrational trade-off. The government ought to remember that it has committed itself to regard the alleviation of poverty as its highest priority.

Another problem with the government's AA policy is the job-hopping by senior public servants that also undermines the efficiency of the state. Amano Edigheij (2007) claims that 'some black managers are preoccupied with searching for the next senior position that is advertised. To stem this tide, at least in the short-run, it might be useful for government to introduce a system whereby senior public officials serve a minimum timeframe before they can move to another job within the public sector.'

Joel Netshitenzhe (*Sunday Times*, 17 June 2012), is rather critical about the manner in which black people in senior positions aspire to achieve the middle class living standards of European countries:

> In pursuit of nonracial equality the black middle and upper strata aspire to achieve [the] high standard of living [of the European middle class]; and many strive to do so in one fell swoop. This has contributed to the [high] levels of inequality in our society. The position of the emergent black middle and upper strata is tenuous and insecure. The consequence of this is that unlike the middle strata in 'mature' class societies, their raison d'étre is not so much pride in the professions, or engagement in discourse on the nation's vision, or the shaping of positive value systems for society. Rather, it is survival and climbing the steep social ladder ... [Consequently] intra-party patronage and corruption take root.

The lack of efficiency in parts of the public sector can also be ascribed to the fact that many black employers are not familiar with the kind of discipline that is essential for employees in a modern society. In modern societies there ought to be several mechanisms – of a religious, a social, a judicial, a political and an economic nature – that reward 'good' behaviour and punish 'bad' behaviour, for if 'good' behaviour is not justly rewarded and 'bad' behaviour is not justly punished, a good order and the promotion of the general well-being would be out of the question. 'Reward-and-punishment' mechanisms should be applicable to everyone in all walks of life. The ANC should be watchful that a culture of *'rewards-without-punishment'* does not become entrenched in its elite circles. It happens that beneficiaries of AA are appointed to positions for which they are not 'suitably qualified' and then commit professional mistakes for which they ought to be penalised in some way or other – but they are often not punished for their mistakes. What is more, they are often not prepared to take punishment or to be reprimanded and are inclined to pardon themselves by claiming that they are the victims of apartheid. Joel Netshitenzhe's article describes this attitude as follows: 'Within society, there develops among rabble rousers a nationalism of convenient victimhood, where racial slogans are used to hide incompetence and greed. The logic in this instance is: because you were oppressed, you can mess up, steal and plunder; and shout "racism!" when challenged.'

To tackle the serious labour problem of poorly schooled black people with very low levels of skills, the ANC government has over the past eighteen years spent billions on black education. Presently more than 20 per cent of the central budget (or R207 billion in the 2012/13 budget) is spent on education. This is laudable. But although the 'input' of money and other resources into the educational system increased quite radically after 1994, the 'output' of educated people with matric and post-matric qualifications has been highly unsatisfactory.[33] The main problem is that many of the teachers in township schools lack the qualifications to be good teachers. The level of absenteeism in township schools is also alarmingly high.

The backlog of blacks in schooling is still far too big. The proportion of working-age population with a degree or higher by race increased to 1993 until 2008 as follows: Africans from 0,5 per cent to 1,5 per cent; coloureds from 0,5 per cent to 2,7 per cent; Indians from 6,7 per cent to 5,5 per cent and whites from 14,2 per cent to 19,6 per cent (Leibrant et al, SALDRU, 2011). From the point of view of human capital formulation, the 'outcomes' of the educational system are a matter of great concern.

chapter six

The Entrenchment and the Intensification of South Africa's social problems: Poverty, Unemployment and Inequality (the PUI problem)

A ll the social evils attached to abject poverty, structural unemployment and growing inequality negatively affect more
or less the same section of the South African population: the
poorest 25 million, of whom 95 per cent are African and 5 per
cent are coloured. The interaction between poverty, unemployment
and inequality (PUI) not only entrenches and aggravates these
people's predicament, but also intensifies the burden of their
deprivation.

South Africa's PUI problem is mainly a remnant of segregation and
apartheid, but has been further intensified by the ANC government's
myopic policy measures to integrate South Africa in too great a
hurry into neoliberal global capitalism and to create – also in too
great a hurry – a new black elite by methods that are detrimental
to the impoverished black majority. The social grants that are paid
to about 25 per cent of the population have made the burden of
poverty more bearable for millions of people. But to give social
grants to about 14 million people in an environment of poverty
in which a further 8 or 10 million people do not receive income
from wages, remittances or social grants has created unforeseen
problems (Leibrant et al, SALDRU, 2011).

Poverty and deprivation

South Africa maintained an annual growth rate of about 4,5 per
cent from 1934 until 1974. During this period the per capita income
of Africans was less than 9 per cent of the per capita income of
whites. From 1974 until 1994 the annual growth rate was a dismal
1,7 per cent annually. In this period the per household income
of the poorer 40 per cent of Africans declined by at least 35 per

cent, while the per household income of the top 20 per cent of Africans increased by more than 35 per cent. After 1994, the per capita income of the poorer 60 per cent of Africans increased as a result of improved social services and social grants. But in spite of the increase in the money and resources at the disposal of the poor, the poorest 50 per cent still received less than 8 per cent of total income in 2008 (Leibrant and Woolard, SALDRU, 2010). Although income poverty of the impoverished majority may have improved since 1994, their socio-economic conditions have deteriorated quite considerably, for several reasons, since 1994.

Poverty is a phenomenon of multiple deprivations. Two dimensions of this multifaceted problem that have become much more severe since the late 1980s are the HIV/AIDS problem and the large-scale migration from the so-called homelands and other African countries to informal settlements around urban areas and larger towns – the 'squatterisation' of millions of people.

It is, of course, not possible to give a full description of the traumatic impact that the HIV/AIDS pandemic has had, and still has, on millions of South Africans. That the life expectancy of South Africans has declined from about sixty years in 1994 to less than fifty years at present is perhaps the best indication of the devastating consequences of the pandemic. The controversy about HIV/AIDS and the non-availability of medicine for those affected are undoubtedly among the darkest stains on the ANC's policy record over the past eighteen years. The pandemic affected more women than men, and also placed a very heavy load on them in their role as caregivers and managers of households. The fact that the health services available for the majority are inadequate has also aggravated the predicament of the poor.

A second phenomenon that has intensified poverty is the large-scale urbanisation of people from rural areas and from other African countries heading to the informal settlements or squatter camps around the cities and large towns. This process started when influx control was abolished in 1986, but accelerated after 1994 when South Africa's borders became much more open. The fact that neither the NP government nor the ANC government has, since 1986, built the necessary infrastructural facilities in the multiple squatter camps, has intensified the poverty of their inhabitants.

The impoverished and mostly unemployed people in the urban informal sector live mostly in extended households. There is a popular perception that if some of the members of an extended household in a squatter camp are receiving social grants, all the members of that extended family can survive. The perception is that if, say, R10 000 is received monthly by certain members of the extended family and put into 'one pot', the fifteen or twenty family members can live a decent life in harmony with each other. Sarah Mosoetsa has done extensive research on the lifestyle in two settlement camps in KwaZulu-Natal. In her excellent little book, *Eating from One Pot* (2011), she comes to the conclusion that life patterns within the extended households are often as conflicting and as violent as the life patterns of the unruly squatter camps in which the extended households are situated. The conflict, the infighting and the violence among the inhabitants of an extended household are mainly about how the available money in the 'one pot' is to be divided and about who gets what. The family members belong to different generations, different age groups and different gender groups, and often not to the same kinship group.

Mosoetsa adapts the idea of cooperative conflict to argue that there is more conflict than cooperation in these households. The interactions between the members of these households are characterised by *unequal* power relations, *unequal* needs and *unequal* desires. The overcrowding and unequal power dynamics often turn the households into war zones in which relentless battles are fought uninterruptedly. Many of these battles are for survival.

It often happened that when the income increased the household would become even more overcrowded as unemployed individuals without any income simply settled in. A great irony about the condition of impoverishment is that children and young people are exposed through the mass media to American consumerism and often fight bitterly to get a part of 'their money' to spend on luxury goods in a situation in which chronic food crises are experienced.

According to Mosoetsa, 'alcohol and drug abuse, and the feeling of powerlessness and shame they produce, contributes to the escalating incidents of domestic abuse and violence in most households. These conflicts limit the potential of households to become viable livelihood sources for vulnerable people.' The inadequate security, the lack of infrastructure and the irregular social services in many of the squatter camps contribute to the misery of life there and the poverty 'mentality' of the inhabitants of the squatter camps is systemically perpetuated from one generation to the next.

It is almost impossible for middle-class people – those who are gated-in behind high walls – to imagine the living pattern of the millions of impoverished South Africans who are living in the extended household war zones within the many war zones in the squatter camp environment. The brokenness and the dangers of the impoverished life in the informal settlements degrade the lives of many poor people to the level of savagery. According to Mosoetsa, however, the extended households 'are not just places of consumption and leisure, but significant places of production and the provision of services ... The unemployment that followed South Africa's entry into the global economy has shifted the focus of survival and economic activity to the household.' It is mainly women who are involved in the household production of goods and services, while men and children are only consumers, which leads to additional conflict and violence within the household and in the broader squatter camp environment. Mosoetsa comes to the general conclusion that the ANC's social policies have failed dismally to alleviate poverty in South Africa:

> South Africa's social and welfare policy framework has not achieved real economic transformation, wealth redistribution or the eradication of poverty. State transfers merely help people to live from hand to mouth. Post-apartheid macroeconomic policies have yielded only limited economic growth while resulting in significant job losses and rising inequality.

What is really disconcerting is that the ANC's attitude towards the poor has changed quite drastically over the past eighteen years. While the poor were regarded in 1994 as the deserving poor who would be the first priority of the ANC government agenda, many in the ANC elite are now inclined to regard the poor as the undeserving poor. The ANC elite often allege that they detect in the behaviour of the poor deficiencies and moral weaknesses that make them slide into dependency, feeding off hand-outs from the state, while doing nothing to help themselves out of poverty (see Everett, 'The undeserving poor', paper read in Moscow, May 2008). Members of the white and the ANC elite warn regularly against the unsustainability of existing social grants, while they protect vigorously the sumptuousness of their own lifestyles as members of the privileged class. What is indeed not sustainable is the large percentage of the population that lives in abject and systemic poverty and the huge gap between the income of the richest 10 million and the poorest 25 million.

In his first speech in parliament on 24 May 1994, President Mandela committed his government to a 'people-centred society', defining it as follows: 'My government's commitment to create a people-centred society of liberty binds us to the pursuit of the goals of freedom from want, freedom from hunger, freedom from deprivation, freedom from ignorance, freedom from suppression and freedom from fear'. Nothing can be further removed from that 'people-centred society' than the PUI problems with which the poor in South Africa are confronted today.

Unemployment and unfree black labour

During the prosperous years from 1934 to 1973 the unemployment problem was restricted to poor white Afrikaners. The supply and mobility of African labour was artificially managed by influx control, while the demand of white entrepreneurs for cheap and docile African labour was almost insatiable. From the early 1970s the unemployment problem became deracialised and from then on it became an ominously bigger problem. In 1970, the labour supply was around 10 million, of whom 8 million were employed. In 1994, the labour supply was around 13 million, of whom 9 million were employed and 4 million (or 31 per cent) unemployed. In 2010, the labour supply increased to around 18 million at least, of whom 13 million were employed and 5 million (or 27 per cent) unemployed. But the potential labour force could have been larger than 20 million in 2010, with 8 to 10 million (or more than 40 per cent) unemployed – the 8 to 10 million individuals who are not receiving wages, remittances or social grants. Whichever figure is used for unemployment, there is no denying the extent of joblessness in South Africa and that job losses continue to mount. Of the 13 million people who were employed in 2010, many are only informally employed. The 'casualisation' of the labour force is exceptionally high among Africans, and a very large percentage of the 8 to 10 million who are unemployed is in the eighteen to thirty age groups. The percentage of GDP that is earned by labour has decreased sharply in relation to the percentage earned by capital since 1994.

The sharp increase in unemployment in the 1970s and 1980s can be ascribed to stagflation and creeping poverty during the struggle years. After job discrimination was abolished at the end of the 1970s, the corporate sector dismissed unskilled workers while its production methods became much more capital intensive. Then, during the 1980s, the agricultural sector started to get rid of a large part of its black labour force and this trend continued after 1994 as the ANC government neglected the white agricultural sector and introduced minimum wages for agricultural workers.

After 1994, two factors led towards a further 'explosion' of un-employment. The first was the adoption of neoliberal globalism and free-trade policies which exposed South Africa to the importation of large quantities of cheaply produced consumer goods mainly from Asian countries where the labour unit cost is much lower than that of South Africa. The second factor that led to greater unemployment was the well-intended labour regulations of the ANC government that have had unforeseen negative consequences. The South African labour legislation embodied in the Labour Relations Act, the Basic Conditions of Employment Act and the Employment Equity Act is far too rigid for a country with the kind of unemployment conditions and labour market segmentations that currently exist in South Africa (see Leibrant et al, SALDRU, 2011). The labour legislation and the rigidity with which it is applied are yet another example of the ANC government's obsession with black elite formation in the upper echelons of the black population and its myopic approach to the detrimental global consequences of such legislation for the rest of the African population group.[34] The South African economy today has much more of a Third World character than it had in 1994. In spite of this situation, the ANC government has enacted labour legislation suited to a First World country and while the new labour legislation has benefitted a small labour elite, it has led to much more unemployment and inequality.

Inequality and the relationship between the rich and the poor

The inequality problem is a more comprehensive problem than those of poverty and unemployment. Inequality in all countries is about the undeserved poverty of the poor vis-à-vis the undeserved wealth of the rich and is therefore about the social injustice in situations in which *systemic* factors enable a small minority of the population to accumulate power and wealth by exploiting a large part of the population and depriving it of property, labour power and opportunities.

There is always a close relationship between the rich and the poor. The rich and the poor are two sides of the same systemic coin. Nothing explains this close relationship better than the situation in South Africa during the first seventy years of the twentieth century when whites constituted 20 per cent of the total population, while receiving more than 70 per cent of total income. Africans constituted almost 70 per cent of the total population, but constantly received less than 20 per cent of the total income – a skewed situation that can be ascribed to the politico-economic system of white political dominance and racial capitalism/corporatism in place in South Africa during that period. In this system both capitalism/corporatism and white political dominance enriched whites undeservedly and impoverished blacks undeservedly (see Terreblanche, 2002).

In neoliberal countries (countries in which the capitalist/corporatist sector is dominant) this close relationship between the rich and the poor is particularly evident. In all neoliberal capitalist countries the poor have gotten poorer since the early 1980s, while the rich have gotten richer. When the system of social democratic capitalism was in place in Western countries in the third quarter of the twentieth century, the democratic governments were powerful enough to tame the capitalist/corporatist sector and to bring about an *equalisation* of income but, when social democratic capitalism was replaced by neoliberal capitalism in the early 1980s, income became much more *unequally* distributed in all Western countries.

In South Africa – before 1994 and after 1994 – the politico-economic systems in place were such that the capitalist/corporatist side always dominated the political side. It is really a pity that the work of the Truth and Reconciliation Commission was not complemented by a *justice and reconciliation commission* tasked to uncover the systemic enrichment and the systemic exploitation and deprivation (or impoverishment) that were brought about by the politico-economic systems that were in place in South Africa from 1894 until 1994, institutionalised by the British empire and supported by Western governments and Western corporations on behalf of the two white (or European) settler groups in South Africa until the late twentieth century.

Why was a justice and reconciliation commission not appointed by the ANC? As indicated above, the elite compromise (or the elite conspiracy) which was agreed upon between the corporate sector and a leadership core of the ANC before 1994 exonerated the white corporations and the white citizens from the part they played in the exploitation and deprivation of blacks, and it also enabled whites to transfer almost all their accumulated wealth, their social and physical wealth – and also the part that was accumulated *undeservedly* – almost intact to the new South Africa. The elite compromise allowed whites to perpetuate their white elitism almost intact. After agreement was reached on the elite compromise, the ANC leadership core was, admittedly, able to implement a policy of black elite formation, but it was deprived of the power to hold white corporations and white citizens accountable for the systemic exploitation and deprivation that was committed by them during the 'century of injustice: 1894-1994' towards black people.[35] Without a justice and reconciliation commission whites would unfortunately never know how extraordinarily advantageous the settlement of 1993/94 has been for most of them.

The ANC government has used the power allotted to it to create a black elite by implementing BEE and AA in rather doubtful and myopic ways, and by plundering the budget recklessly. The perpetuation of white elitism and white corporatism after 1994 and the creation of black elitism over the past eighteen years, to the detriment of the poor and unemployed, can be regarded as the main reasons *why income has become increasingly unequally distributed since 1994*. Over the past eighteen years the Gini coefficient increased from 0,66 to 0,70. The richest 10 million South Africans received almost 75 per cent of total income in 2008, while the poorest 25 million received less than 8 per cent (Leibrant el al, SALDRU, 2010).

The extreme inequality in the distribution of income in South Africa makes it necessary for South Africans to be reminded of Arthur Okun's (1975) 'leaking bucket experiment'. Okun acknowledges that when redistribution takes place water is taken from the relatively full tanks of the rich and transferred to the relatively empty tanks of the poor. The transfer of water from the full to the empty tanks always happens, according to Okun, with buckets that leak. Some of the water is wasted on the ground. Redistribution is a messy business. Okun's argument is, however, that where income is as unequally distributed as in all countries in the world it does not matter if some efficiency is a trade-off for more equality. With this kind of trade-off between equality and efficiency the general well-being of society at large can be increased quite considerably.

Let us take a South African example. If five percentage points of the richest 20 per cent income is transferred with a 'leaky bucket' to the poor, the income of the rich would decline by 6 per cent, while the income of the poor would increase by more than 60 per cent, but because of the leaky buckets the advantage to the poor would be smaller. But it cannot be denied that such a redistribution of income – from the top 20 per cent to the lower 50 per cent – would boost the general well-being of South Africans and is unavoidable if we want to create a humane and civilised society in South Africa. The more unequally income is distributed in a country, the larger the increase in the general well-being if water is transferred from the 'full tanks' of the rich to the 'empty tanks' of the poor.

That South Africa has one of the most unequal – if not the most unequal – distributions of income in the world can be ascribed to the fact that the country has never had a politico-economic system in place in which the political side was powerful enough to tame the capitalist/corporatist side of the dual system; it was also not powerful enough to equalise the distribution of income as happened in Western countries during the third quarter of the twentieth century. Instead of a social democratic system and an equalisation of income since 1994, South Africa has, over the past eighteen years, *experienced an American-led neoliberal transition that empowered the capitalist/corporatist 'side' of our dual system to orchestrate even greater inequalities in the distribution of South Africa's domestic income.*

In spite of the close relationship between wealth and poverty in all neoliberal capitalist countries, the rich are usually not prepared to acknowledge that they are rich because the majority is poor. The rich usually live in denial about the causal relationship between wealth and poverty. They don't like to be the flipside of the poor. The rich are always very self-assured, very complacent and very arrogant about their wealth. They are always of the opinion that what belongs to them does so because of their merit, inventiveness, and perseverance, and that nobody – but nobody – has the right to take it from them. In the South African case, the role that political and economic power constellations have played in the (artificial) enrichment of whites in the century before 1994, and in the (artificial) enrichment of the elite since 1994, is so obvious

111

that it is not necessary to argue the point. We are confronted in South Africa with a serious poverty problem. We are at the same time also confronted with a serious opulence problem.

Amartya Sen (2006) describes the lack of trustworthiness of market prices and of the distribution of income by market forces as follows:

> There is an oddly common presumption that there is such a thing as 'the market outcome', no matter what rules of private operations, public initiatives, and non-market institutions are combined with the existence of markets ... [This presumption] is entirely mistaken. Use of the market economy is consistent with many different ownership patterns, resource availabilities, and rules of operation ... *And depending on these conditions, the market economy itself would generate distinct sets of prices, terms of trade, income distributions, and more generally, very different overall outcomes* [my italics].

Sen's argument is that market prices and the distribution of income always depend on the enabling conditions that are of a social, economic and political nature. In a capitalist system the enabling conditions of capitalism are always such that prices in goods and in factor markets can easily be 'twisted' in favour of those in a position of power, in favour of those with large amounts of marketable assets (both physical and human assets) and in favour of those who have access to the instruments of political power and mass propaganda. The rich and the powerful are always in a stronger position to influence the stream of information and also in a stronger position to spread misinformation – mainly through consumerism. The unequal distribution of power and property are, therefore, responsible for an asymmetry of information that distorts the outcome of markets and the inequalities in the distribution of domestic incomes. Sen's argument is that the enabling conditions of capitalism are always such that income becomes more unequally distributed if capitalism is left to its own devices. Given the unequal distribution of property and power in a capitalist system, the capitalists are always in a position to mercilessly exploit the asymmetric property and power relations for their own enrichment and it is therefore always necessary for governments to implement comprehensive redistribution policies in capitalist countries.

The relationship between government power and corporate power plays an important role in the unequal distribution of domestic income in the United States. In 1928, the richest 1 per cent received 23,5 per cent of total income. Roosevelt's New Deal policy and the social democratic approach in the post-war world reduced the share of the richest 1 per cent to 9 per cent in 1976. After Reagan's neoliberal counter-revolution on behalf of the corporate sector, the share of the richest 1 per cent increased again, to almost 24 per cent in 2008. From 1976 until 2008, the share of the poorest 50 per cent in the US declined from 17 per cent to 12 per cent (*New York Times*, 9 April 2011).

When the system of social democratic capitalism was in place in Western countries in the third quarter of the twentieth century, the democratic governments were powerful enough to tame the capitalist/corporatist sector and to bring about a considerable equalisation of income, but when social democratic capitalism was replaced by neoliberal capitalism in the early 1980s income became much more *unequally* distributed in *all* Western countries. If we study carefully the equality/inequality trends in the US and in Europe over the past eighty years it becomes apparent that government policy is playing a much more important role in determining the level of individual income than the alleged merit or demerit of individuals. When government policy is friendly towards the capitalist elite, income becomes more unequally distributed. When government policy pursues the welfare of society at large, income becomes more equally distributed.

According to George Monbiot (*The Guardian*, 8 November 2011) the rich are always inclined to the self-attribution fallacy. That is, they are always inclined to credit themselves with outcomes for which they were not responsible. Monbiot continues: 'Many of those that are rich today got there because they were able to capture certain jobs. This capture owes less to talent and intelligence than to a combination of the ruthless exploitation of others and accidents of birth, as such jobs are taken disproportionally by people born in certain places and into certain classes.'

In the South African case both the rich whites and the rich blacks are guilty of the self-attribution fallacy. Perhaps we need a justice and reconciliation commission to examine power relations over the past 120 years in order to infuse the necessary degree of humility among the old white elite and the new black elite. It is important that the rich in South Africa should be informed about the important role 'skewed' political and corporate power constellations played in their opulence.

The inequality gap between the very rich and the very poor in South Africa are so monstrously big that it is necessary to reflect on the luxurious and extravagant lifestyle that many of the very rich permit themselves in comparison with the lifestyle the very poor are doomed to live.[36] When the conspicuous consumption, the wastefulness, the greediness and the arrogance of the very rich are judged against the misery and deprivation of so many poor people, then we have no alternative but to be shocked at the vulgarity and the repulsiveness of the lifestyle of the rich. Are the rich and the poor really citizens of the same South Africa?

Is it not time to bring about a Codesa on why so many people are so excessively *too rich* and why even more people are so hopelessly *poor*? The churches played a strategic role in the struggle against apartheid. Why are the churches not conducting an open war on behalf of those that are undeservedly poor and against those that are undeservedly rich?

chapter seven

The Fairy-tale optimism of the National Development plan versus the likelihood that the PUI problem will be perpetuated

It is eighteen years since the momentous transition of 1994. In another eighteen it will be 2030. What will the next eighteen years bring for the poorer part of the South African population? Will it be a 'virtuous' cycle of expanding opportunities, building capabilities and poverty reduction? Or will the downward spiral of the PUI problem that has occurred since 1973 be perpetuated for another eighteen years at least?

The National Planning Commission (2011) formulates the main task in its National Development Plan (NDP) as follows:

> The National Plan has to attack the plight of poverty and exclusion, and [promote] economic growth at the same time, creating a virtuous cycle of expanding opportunities, building capacities, reducing poverty, involving communities in their own development, all leading to rising living standards.

The main targets of the Commission are to reduce the proportion of the people living below the level of R418 (at 2009 figures) from the current 39 per cent of the population to zero, and to reduce the unemployment rate from 27 per cent in 2011 to 6 per cent in 2030 by creating an additional eleven million jobs. If these targets and the other targets set by the Commission can be accomplished by 2030 it would be an excellent accomplishment. But who is going to implement the policy measures that will be necessary in order to realise the hyper-optimistic targets set by the NDP? Who is going to equalise the unequal power relations, the *unequal* property distribution and the *unequal* opportunities that must be put right before the NDP targets can be attained.

To compile a comprehensive list of targets as the Commission has done is, perhaps, a valuable exercise to spotlight the many things that are wrong in South Africa's politico-economic system. But this kind of exercise is valueless if the targets are compiled without spelling out the institutional changes – *and the changes in the power and property relations* – that would have to be in place before the South African politico-economic system can become functional to serve the interests of the total population instead of the narrow class interests of the capitalists and political elite, as has been the case from 1886 until 1994, and over the past eighteen years.

The Commission is putting its trust in a 'new story' that has to be written in the years ahead and the purpose of which is to create 'a virtuous cycle of expanding opportunities'. The NDP continues:

> Such a virtuous cycle requires agreement across society about the contribution and sacrifices of all sectors and interests ... *In the new story every citizen is concerned about the wellbeing of all other citizens*, and the development of South Africa means the development of each and every one of us who lives here. We must build on our social solidarity, which, through history and heritage, has demonstrated our aspirations to create a caring South African society [my emphasis].

I have serious problems in understanding the meaning of this quotation from the NDP. Both the quotation, and the whole trend, of the NDP's thinking seem to me rather superficial and naïve. The paragraph quoted above sounds to me like religious sentimentalism, or the sermon of a lay preacher. If everyone is to make sacrifices and become concerned about the well-being of all citizens, does this also include the greedy billionaires who allot themselves R200 or R300 million as remuneration every year?

Does it mean that nobody would any longer pursue self-interest but would be inspired to create a caring South African society? For those who are really concerned about the structural nature of South Africa's PUI problem it all sounds rather airy-fairy. How is it possible that an important government Commission can keep itself busy with such airy-fairy stuff, while 25 million South Africans are trapped in a systemic condition of abject poverty, increasing unemployment and growing inequality?

Why has the Commission not concentrated on the unequal power relations, the unequal property relations and the unequal opportunities that are making the new South Africa society a very unjust society – just as similar inequalities made apartheid South Africa a very unjust place in which to live? Why is the Commission not concentrating on addressing the wrong power shifts that took place during the transformation process and which have not only perpetuated but also actually aggravated social injustice in South Africa? We could have expected the Commission to formulate *concrete, practical* and *implementable* policy measures to solve our most serious predicament, the PUI problem. But instead of such policy measures the Commission is concerned mainly about the many targets that should be reached by 2030. If all these 'shoulds' stipulated in the NDP become realities in 2030 it would be excellent. But what *should* be done to change what *is* in 2012 into what *should be* in 2030? As long as the National Planning Commission fails to provide concrete answers as to how these targets are going to be met, all the goals in the NDP will remain fairy-tale targets. With this kind of wishful thinking the plight of the poor and the unemployed will remain unresolved – and could become even more severe.

The main problem with the NDP is that it has not considered the historic trends of the past 130 years and it does not consider the structural nature of our PUI problem, the role political and economic power structures have played from 1886 to 1994, and since 1994, in creating and perpetuating the PUI problem.

I was born in 1933. I will be eighty years old in 2013. The first half of my life was a very prosperous period. The annual growth rate was higher than 4 per cent and per capita income grew by almost 3 per cent. In biblical terms these were the forty fat years. All population groups benefitted, but the Afrikaners benefitted the most. While the Afrikaner poor white problem was severe in 1933, it had for all practical purposes been resolved by 1973 as a consequence of the dramatic rise of the Afrikaners to the middle class. The Afrikaners used and misused their political power and their growing partnership with the rich English establishment to solve their poverty problem – unfortunately to the detriment of the black population.

The twenty years from 1973 until 1993 were in biblical terms the twenty lean years. This was a period of stagflation and growing unemployment. The annual economic growth rate was only 1,7 per cent, while the annual population growth rate was 2,5 per cent. Amid creeping poverty, the per household income of the top 20 per cent of the black population increased sharply, while the per household income of the top 20 per cent of the whites changed very little. But during this period of creeping poverty the per household income of the poorest 40 per cent of all population groups (except Asians) declined quite sharply (see Terreblanche, 2002: Table 10.4).

The annual economic growth rate in the eighteen years since 1994 has been about 3,5 per cent. This growth rate is quite satisfactory when compared to that of the previous twenty years. But the PUI problem became more severe since 1994 as a consequence of the unequal power relations that were institutionalised when the elite compromise embraced the ideologies of neoliberal globalism and market fundamentalism in 1993/94.

The richest 10 per cent of the population benefitted the most in this period. Their share of total income increased from 53,9 per cent in 1993 to 58,1 per cent in 2008. The portion of blacks amongst the richest 10 per cent became larger, while they also became richer. The income of the next richest 10 per cent declined from 17,7 per cent in 1993 to 16,6 per cent in 2008. The income of the poorest 50 per cent declined from 8,4 per cent in 1993 to 7,8 per cent in 2008 (Leibrant et al; SALDRU, 2010).

Since the early 1970s, the poorest 50 per cent of the population has been exposed to a vicious circle – or a downward spiral – of growing poverty, growing unemployment and growing inequality. The power relations in place in South Africa in the forty years from 1973 until 2012 were such that the vicious downward spiral in which the poorest 50 per cent were trapped was perpetuated. It was like a snowball rolling down a steep mountain and building up momentum as it rolled, and there are no signs whatsoever that the ANC government can implement measures to stop this rolling snowball in its tracks. If we take the Great Recession and the serious debt problems of the United States and Europe into account and consider the possibility that the American-led neoliberal empire can squeeze its neocolonial satellites in the global South (South Africa included) for a larger 'imperial dividend' to repay its huge debts, the possibility exists that the downward spiral of the PUI problem can be perpetuated with even greater force for the next decade or two.

The growing severity of the PUI problem since 1994 should be blamed on the elite compromise that put local and foreign corporations in extraordinarily powerful positions. After neoliberalism and market fundamentalism were embraced in 1996, and when it was decided that taxation and expenditure would remain a fixed proportion of GDP, it was not possible for the ANC government to implement a comprehensive redistribution policy. The elite compromise created the space for black elite formation, but not for a policy that would alleviate the poverty of the poorest 50 per cent in a meaningful way.

On page 416 of the NDP, the Commission asks the following important question on 'righting the wrongs of the past':

> How does South Africa break [the vicious] cycle and enter a more virtuous one of rising confidence, investment, employment and incomes, and falling levels of inequality? Given the country's history of lacking confidence, *[the ANC] government needs to provide the catalyst for the virtuous cycle to begin* ... Removing the obstacles to faster economic growth, increasing the pace of investment in infrastructure, improving service delivery (especially quality education) and building confidence [the ANC government] would provide the *impetus* for the private sector to invest and to take a long-term perspective when it invests [my emphasis].

The above statement is truly a shocking one. The whole of the NDP boils down to the ANC government's task to 'remove the obstacles to faster economic growth ... [and] building confidence'. But for several reasons the ANC government is part of the problem and cannot, therefore, be part of the solution. In our new politico-economic system the ANC government and the ANC-controlled bureaucracy are far too weak and far too myopic – and also far too corrupt – to take the initiative in the planning of a developmental state, and they have not, in any case, the capacity to call the capitalist /corporatist sector effectively to account.

It is also not realistic to expect that the capitalist/corporatist sector would take the initiative in what the NDP describes as 'a virtuous cycle of expanding opportunities'. Although the corporate sector is a dogmatic propagandist of market fundamentalism, it is organised in conglomerates (like the MEC) and in globally orientated oligopolistic giants. The capitalist/corporatist sector is *only* interested in promoting its rather narrow class interest and is definitely not concerned about 'the well-being of all other citizens' as the NDP wants them to be. The economic growth that has been attained over the past eighteen years was very profitable for the corporate sector, but it has an undeniable 'trickle-up effect', and since 1997 the corporate sector has become 'globally mobile' to such an extent that it is in any case not interested in taking the initiative envisaged by the NDP. In the eventuality of a decline of profitability in South Africa, a large part of the capitalist/corporatist sector is likely to move on to global markets.

Owing to the malfunctioning of our new politico-economic system, there exists no chance whatsoever that the multiple (and beautiful-sounding) targets of the NDP will be reached in the next twenty years. It is much more likely that the PUI problem will be more severe in 2030 than it is today.

When reading the NDP (and being overwhelmed by the multiplicity of targets set for 2030), one cannot but be suspicious. The members of the NPC ought to know that it is not possible to reach all the targets it has set by 2030. Why has the NPC formulated so many targets with such sincerity if they cannot be realised in time? I suspect that the NDP is actually a carefully crafted ideological propaganda document.

This version of ideological propaganda could be called the 'ideology of targetism'. The aim of this ideological propaganda is to lull the general public, and especially the impoverished majority, into contentment until 2030. If only the poor and the unemployed were prepared to live their heavy ordeal until 2030, they were given the assurance by the NPC that, when the sun rises over South Africa on the morning of 1 January 2030, it would be a bright morning, and South Africa would be a fabulous country without poverty and with only 6 per cent unemployment! Let nobody rock the boat and let everyone await the first of January 2030, when our social problems will vanish with the morning sun!

Important stumbling blocks en route to a solution of the PUI problem are the Americanisation of the South African economy and the power and property that were allocated to the local and foreign corporate sectors by the elite compromise of 1993/94. How is the ANC government going to remove these obstacles? What is the NDP planning to do about the excessive power concentrated in the hands of the corporate conglomerates and oligopolistic giants? Is it going to 'de-Americanise' the South African economy? Is it going to 'deglobalise' the South African firms that were given the privilege of shifting their listings to London and New York? Is it going to 'de-Africanise' the bureaucracy in an attempt to restore some of its erstwhile effectiveness and efficiency? Is it going to hold all the South African corporations that enriched themselves undeservedly during the apartheid years accountable for the exploitation of unfree black labour? Is it going to implement a comprehensive redistributive policy? If the ANC government is not going to do these things to reach its hyper-optimistic targets, what is it going to do?

chapter eight

What went wrong in the Transformation Process 1986-2012?

It is already twenty-five years since the transformation process started in 1986, and time for South Africans to acknowledge, in all sincerity, that the transformation has been a disappointing one – a huge failure, in fact. We replaced the immoral and inhumane system of apartheid with an immoral and inhumane politico-economic system. The political 'side' of the new dual system is pathetically inefficient and corrupt, while the economic 'side' is too powerful, too self-centered and too globally orientated. It is time for South Africans – black and white – to ask penetrating questions about what went wrong during the transformation process. Let us summarise some of the obvious failures.

- We did not succeed in properly addressing the apartheid legacy of abject poverty, high unemployment and growing inequality. On the contrary. The PUI problem is today more severe than it was during apartheid.
- We succeeded in getting rid of the immoral and inhumane system of apartheid, but we did not succeed in putting a moral and humane system in its place. The post-apartheid period is in many aspects as immoral and as inhumane as the apartheid period – if not more so. The white elite and the white corporations were given the privilege of transferring all the wealth they had accumulated in the apartheid period – and also the part that was accumulated undeservedly – almost intact to the new South Africa. Most of them have enriched themselves quite handsomely over the past eighteen years, while the attitude of many whites is conspicuously indifferent to the plight of the

impoverished majority. For the new black corporations, lucrative opportunities have been created since 1994 to accumulate considerable wealth, and part of their wealth was also *undeservedly* accumulated. One gets the impression that the the new black elite and the new black corporations are also conspicuously indifferent towards the plight of the impoverished majority. We might have expected that those who were fortunate enough to board the gravy train would display more empathy with those who were not as fortunate. Sadly, this is obviously not the case.

- One of the most perturbing aspects of the post-apartheid period is the adoption among a large part of the new black elite of an extravagant get-rich-quick mentality and their consequent preparedness to use immoral and devious methods. They display not only the typical behaviours of a *nouveau riche bourgeoisie* but also the behaviour of Mammon worshipers. Are they imitating the example set by a very rich white elite?

- One of the most serious things that has gone wrong in the post-apartheid period is that, while all blacks should have benefitted from black economic empowerment, only a tiny minority have been economically empowered, and the alarming gap that has opened up between the small African elite and the almost 24 million Africans who are among the 25 million poorest in South Africa, receiving less than 8 per cent of total income. It is a gap with revolutionary implications.

- We did not succeed in creating the 'people-centred society' envisaged by President Mandela in May 1994, and neither did we succeed in creating the 'rainbow nation' envisaged by Archbishop Tutu.

- In 2002, I explored South Africa's modern history from the perspective of unequal power relations and unfree (black) labour patterns. In spite of the process of democratisation, the outstanding feature of post-apartheid South Africa is the perpetuation of unequal power relations between the non-racial elite and the lumpen proletariat, while unfree labour manifests itself in growing unemployment in a socio-economic environment in which up to 10 million people do not receive wages, or any form of remittance or social grants.

- We did not succeed in replacing the deeply divided South African society of the apartheid period with a society of social solidarity and proud South Africanism. On the contrary. After transformation South Africa is still very much a divided society with new kinds of cleavages within and between different ethnic and racial population groups. Although most whites benefitted from a rather advantageous 'deal' during the transformation, many of them are – curiously enough – not prepared to acknowledge the multiple injustices that were committed by them or on their behalf towards blacks during 'the century of injustice'. Many whites lament that they are 'sick and tired' of being reminded of their apartheid debt, but what they apparently do not realise is that it will still be justifiable, for decades to come, to remind them of what is still unpaid.

- The politico-economic system that was in place during the apartheid years was dominated by the MEC and the rest of the corporate sector. The politico-economic system in place in the post-apartheid period is to an even greater degree dominated by the MEC and other local and foreign corporations. The apartheid ugly ducklings were supposedly transformed into beautiful corporative swans, but the swans are as exploitative of unfree black labour and as guilty of all kinds of negative ecological externalities as was the case during the apartheid period – if not more so. Capitalism/corporatism is monopolising power in South Africa, to the detriment of the majority. It is of utmost importance that the wings of corporatism be clipped.

- After forty fat years in biblical terms from 1933 until 1973, when the Afrikaners experienced their rise to the bourgeoisie, South Africa's poorest 50 per cent experienced forty lean years in biblical terms. From 1973 until 1994 they experienceed twenty lean years in biblical terms. From 1994 to 2012 they experienced another twenty lean years during the period of globalised corporatism. In the 'forty years' from 1974 to 2012 the PUI problem has become much more severe.

- Most of the many things that went wrong during the transformation process seem to be related to the elite compromise/conspiracy. We experienced a major power shift in the mid-1990s, but it seems as if the terms on which the reconfiguration of power has taken place were wrong. According to the proverb, *the iron should be struck while it is hot*, the iron was indeed hot in the early 1990s but it was struck into the wrong shape. Too much power and too many privileges were given to the South African corporations; too much power and too many privileges were given to transnational corporations, too much power and too many privileges were given to the emerging black corporations; while only restricted power was given to the ANC government itself – and the power given to the ANC government was restricted by the conditionalities that it had to maintain fiscal austerity and deficit reduction, and that taxation and expenditure must be pegged as fixed proportions of GDP. The ANC government was bribed and corrupted at the same time. The fiscal authority that was allotted to the ANC government was too restricted to enable it to implement a comprehensive redistribution policy, but large enough for black elite formation. As a consequence, the ANC government has done far too little for the impoverished black majority and far too much for the emerging black elite.

Perhaps the ANC government can be convinced to come to their senses about the implications of being integrated into the structures of global capitalism/corporatism and about the implications of being a neocolonial satellite of the American-led neoliberal empire. When I emphasise the need to take the (hostile) global environment into consideration when policy decisions are made, it does not imply that I am in agreement with global capitalism/corporatism or with the behaviour of the American-led neoliberal empire. In fact, I detest the global environment into which the elite compromise of 1993 integrated the South African politico-economic system.

The ANC government was, right from the beginning, not sufficiently aware of its restricted sovereignty. In the past eighteen years it has not acted with the necessary circumspection about South Africa's vulnerable position as a relative poor and developing state in a hostile global environment. The ANC has regularly taken decisions that were mercilessly punished by global capitalism/corporatism and by the conditionalities of the Washington Consensus. The ANC government has, in the past eighteen years, been too obsessed with black elite formation, with irresponsible BEE and AA contracts and with setting a labour pattern that is too rigid for a country with such high levels of unemployment. But what is really disconcerting, is that South Africa's restricted sovereignty of 1994 has shrunk quite considerably over the past five years, mainly as a consequence of the Great Recession, the serious debt crises of the US and Europe and the staggering arrogance of Western transnational corporations in the emerging mercantilistic struggle between Western corporations and the equally arrogant corporations of the BRICS nations. Is South Africa running the risk that it is going to be crushed by the competition between the Western and the BRICS countries?

It is high time that the ANC realises its own limitations and the limitations of South Africa and high time for the ANC to acquire some humility and try to govern with *governance*, *transparency*, fairness and without *squandering money*. Is there a chance that this is going to happen? I doubt it.

Because the reconfiguration of power that took place in the early 1990s happened in the wrong way, we have apparently no other choice but to wait until the socio-economic and political situation in South Africa and internationally has deteriorated to such a degree that the 'systemic iron' becomes hot enough once again to be struck in a different and better shape, for the socio-economic crisis in South Africa is already so serious that it has already become imperative to bring about a radical (new) transformation.

But we also run the danger that when the 'systemic iron' heats up again the situation could turn out to be so precarious that a traumatic 'systemic derailment' could take place.

When will the socio-economic and the political situation again become so bad that the 'systemic iron' will be hot enough to be hammered into a better shape? Nobody knows – it's anyone's guess. But we should not delude ourselves into thinking that it is going to be in the remote rather than the more immediate future. The more recalcitrant and the more myopic the small, enriched elite with huge vested interest in the present dispensation becomes, the greater the danger that the next 'systemic crisis' will turn out to be a massive derailment of the system, rather than an opportunity to improve it.

Notes

Introduction

[1] See Terreblanche (2002) for the secret negotiations that took place in the early 1990s on the future economic system of South Africa.

Chapter one

[2] According to Chalmers Johnson (2004: 56), Reagan sharply increased the military spending of the US in the early 1980s. Huge investments were made in weapons systems like the B-2 stealth bomber, and in high-tech research and development, for his strategic defence initiative or 'Star Wars', the funds for which were largely hidden in the Pentagon's 'black budget'. The development enhanced the US military capability quite dramatically vis-à-vis the Soviet Union.

[3] Reagan and Gorbachev met five times: in Geneva in 1985; in Reykjavik in October 1986; in Washington in December 1987; in Moscow in May 1988; and in New York in December 1988 (in the company of the newly elected President George Bush). The meeting at Reykjavik was the most important of the five meetings.

[4] When the massacre on Tiananmen square in Beijing took place on 3-4 June 1989, Gorbachev told the Soviet troops still stationed in eastern European countries to remain in their barracks if similar uprisings were to occur in those countries. This was an acknowledgement that the Brezhnev doctrine was no longer applicable. Gorbachev's attitude facilitated the fall of the Berlin Wall in 1989.

Chapter two

[5] The process of integrating Western Europe into the framework of the American empire started with the Atlantic Charter, which

was agreed upon between the United States and Britain in 1941. At the Bretton Woods conference (1944) it was decided to create the International Monetary Fund to stabilise exchange rates and the flow of international capital and the World Bank to support economic revival in Western Europe. The rest of the institutional framework of the Western Club – with West-West interdependence and European dependence on the United States – was created in the five years after 1945. The most important of these institutions were the United Nations, NATO, the Marshall Aid Plan and GATT.

[6] Victoria de Gracia (2005: 345-6) alleges 'that the imprint [of the Marshall Plan] lays not so much in its financial contribution to European reconstruction as in the *conditions* that were demanded to disburse the aid ... [The Marshall Plan] aimed at building a self-sustained industrialised Europe, one that thrived by intra-regional trade yet was firmly inserted into the American-dominated world economy ... Consequently, the first priority of [financial] aid was to boost productivity by investing in industrial retooling and in infrastructure'.

[7] The post-war boom came to an end in the late 1960s at a time when increased competition took place between Western countries in the procurement of industrial inputs and in the disposal of industrial outputs in world markets; this led to a decline in profitability and to upward pressures on the purchase prices of primary products. A first manifestation of this upward pressure was the 'pay explosion' that took place from 1968 to 1973 when real wages rose much faster than labour productivity and thereby provoked a major decline in corporate profits. A second manifestation of upward pressure in input cost was the 'oil shocks' of 1973 and 1979 (see Arrighi, 1994: 303-310).

[8] The financial speculation during the first financialisation of the global economy ultimately led to the collapse of global capitalism of London and the financial centre of the world in 1931. A first

financialisation of the global economy was experienced in Britain during the high point of Victorian globalisation in the decades before the First World War.

[9] Colás and Saull (2006: 1-8) described the USA's dominant position in the system of 'closed frontiers and open markets' as follows: 'Wherever … closed frontiers and open markets were threatened … Washington projected its coercive global power in an attempt to shore up state authority and capitalist social relations. The USA had – and arguably continues to have – various resources in the pursuit of such aims: as the largest capitalist economy, it had the compulsion of the market on its side; as the leading capitalist state it enjoyed the authority to coordinate other capital states, as a military and nuclear superpower it was [and still is] able to deploy unsurpassed legal force by land, air, sea and eventually space'.

[10] Chalmers Johnson (2004: 188 and 23-26) describes the American-led global empire as an empire 'of military bases'. The US maintained military bases in almost every corner of the globe. Johnson puts it as follows: 'What is most fascinating and curious about the developing of the American form of empire … is that, in its modern phase, *it is solely an empire of bases, not of territories*, and these bases now encircle the earth in a way that, despite centuries old dreams of global domination, would previously have been inconceivable … Whatever the original reason the United States entered a country and set up a base, *it remained for imperial reasons*'.

[11] The claims of the ideologues of market-fundamentalism are so outrageous that Harvey Cox (*The Atlantic Monthly*, March, 1991) has ridiculed that they are alleviating the Market to the position of God. He puts it as follows: 'In Christianity, God has sometimes been defined as omnipotent (possessing all power), omniscient (having all knowledge), and omnipresent (existing everywhere). Most Christian theologies, it is true, hedge a bit. They teach that

these qualities of the divinity are indeed *there*, but are hidden from human eyes both by human sin and by the transcendence of the divine itself ... Likewise, although the Market, we are assured, possesses these divine attributes, they are not always completely evident to mortals *but must be trusted and affirmed by faith [in market-fundamentalism]*'

Chapter three

[12] Lester Thurow (1996: 17-18) describes the rise and the fall of democratic capitalism as follows: 'Human societies need a vision of something better. By definition utopias cannot be built, but they provide elements that can be built into our current, less than perfect economic systems ... Where are the visions of better human societies from? ... *Democracy believes in one man, one vote' (equality* of political power), while *capitalism* believes in letting the market rule (in practice great *inequalities* in economic power). In [the third quarter of] the twentieth century this ideological conflict between the *equalitarian* foundations of democracy and the *inequalitarian* realty of capitalism has been finessed by the crafting of social investments and the social welfare state onto capitalism and democracy ... But [in the recent past] social investment such as education are being crowded out of government budgets to pay for pension and health benefits for the elderly. The ideology of [social] inclusion is withering away, to be replaced by a *revival of survival-of-the-fittest* [or neoliberal capitalism]'. [my italics]

[13] The VOC was recently identified, along with Ford Motors and Microsoft, as the three corporations that influenced human life the most (see Sleigh D, *Die Burger*, 28.12.2009).

[14] The Dutch became notorious among other European nations for the fact that neither moral nor religious principles prevented them from making profits. During the Eighty Years War (1568-1648)

Dutch ships regularly traded in Spanish harbours. When a Dutchman was reprimanded about his business practices, his answer was that 'if he could make a commercial profit by passing through hell, he would risk burning the sails of his ships in doing so' (quoted by Boxer, 1966: 113). Are some South African businessmen perpetuating this Dutch tradition?

[15] During the Anglo-Boer War the British government was guilty – on behalf of the gold mining industry – of genocide against the Afrikaner inhabitants of the two Boer Republics. While other European empires committed genocide against non-Europeans in the non-European world, Britain was the only European empire that committed genocide against European settlers in the non-European world. More than 10 per cent of the Afrikaner inhabitants of the two Boer Republics were killed during the Anglo-Boer War. This represents an abnormally high percentage of war death and reflects negatively on British greed and savagery. This happened at the height of Victorian imperial arrogance, when the sustainability of the British empire was being seriously challenged by industrialisation in Germany and the US (see Stephen Howe, 2000: 75-76, Herfried Münkler, 2007: 127-128; Paul Kennedy, 1988: 195-392).

[16] It is rather strange that the powerful 'mining press' relentlessly criticised the *discriminatory* legislation that was enacted on behalf of the Afrikaners, but never complained about the repressive labour legislation that lowered the cost of black labour to the advantage of the mainly English-speaking corporate sector. Harry Oppenheimer and Helen Suzman were in the 1950s and 1960s extraordinary critical of the discriminatory measure to protect Afrikaners at a time when the repressive labour on behalf of the mainly English-speaking corporate sector was still on the law books. I am not aware of any criticism by either Oppenheimer or Suzman of the repressive and exploitative labour legislation.

[17] Dan O'Meara (1996: 81) describes the reaction of the white English-speakers to the apartheid government as follows: 'The NP's apartheid policies created the conditions for rapid accumulation of capital ... Apartheid thus proved to be good for every white's business. Whatever their moral and theoretical qualms about NP racial policy, I [i.e. O'Meara] know of no Anglophone liberal businessman who declined to profit from this NP 'interference' in the 'free market', and raise their [black] workers' wages'. Was the English establishment in South Africa as hypocritical as the English at the core of the British empire?

[18] The deal was vehemently opposed by conservative (or *verkrampte*) Afrikaners with the argument that Afrikaners were selling their soul to English/British capitalist/imperialistic power. The rapprochement between Afrikaner and English corporations triggered the relentless battle in Afrikaner circles that would rage on for the next thirty years between the *verligte* (enlightened) and *verkrampte* (conservative) Afrikaners on business issues, but especially on matters regarding the future position of black – and especially African – people in South Africa.

[19] As was the case of Britain – which had been involved in almost a hundred wars since 1689 – the books of the Department of Defence were not audited by the auditor general.

Chapter four

[20] De Beer also declared in his interview that the 'politicisation' of Cosatu (in 1985) was an additional reason why it became necessary for business to play an active political role: 'Cosatu has a more articulate political leadership than any of its predecessors ... [Cosatu's militancy] put management into a political frontline where it doesn't belong and doesn't want to be ... Businessmen get very angry with that sort of thing. They regard it as unfair ... Business is

more than irritated by the political tone of a great many of these unions ... Nevertheless, senior business leadership everywhere is determined to try to make the new industrial relations set-up work'.

[21] The success attained by the three 'independent' candidates in the election was a huge setback for the so-called Cape Liberal (or *verligte*) wing of the NP. The Cape Liberals blamed their inability to make progress with reform on the recalcitrant attitude of the conservative (or *verkrampte*) wing of the NP in the Transvaal. When the Discussion Group '85 challenged the Cape Liberals on the issue of negotiation with the ANC, it became apparent that the *'verligtheid'* of the Cape Liberals was actually only skin deep. PW Botha, Chris Heunis and Piet Cilliers (of Naspers) were prepared to 'share power' with the coloureds and Indians in the Tricameral Parliament, but when we confronted them with the challenge of sharing power with the ANC, they refused bluntly and responded angrily. The 1987 election undermined the legitimacy of Botha and Heunis quite seriously.

[22] When I expressed my wish in the Leadership article in 1987 that the NP should crumble into pieces, I could not have dreamed that the NP would 'dissolve' into non-existence within fifteen years.

[23] FW de Klerk, the then new leader of the NP, has to take full responsibility for the NP's doubtful election campaign of 1989. The NP was at the time panic-stricken that the election could result in a 'hung parliament', if the DP and the Conservative Party together won more seats than the NP. On 2 February 1990, FW de Klerk made his big 'reform speech' in which he used many of the arguments that were put forward in the March 1987 declaration of Discussion Group 85 and in the Election Manifesto of the DP.

[24] Although I was involved in the 'talks about talks' in the period from 1987 until 1989, I was never involved in the negotiation process from 1990 until 1994. I have been told that at the time

senior individuals attached to the Sanlam Group of corporations were very much against my involvement, because of my preference for a system of social democratic capitalism and because of the emphasis I put on the need for a comprehensive redistribution policy to address the inequalities of apartheid.

[25] I gave evidence before the Truth and Reconciliation Commission on 11 November 1997. In my evidence I proposed a wealth tax on whites to build a restitution fund that should be used for the alleviation of severe black poverty. I was of the opinion that the *symbolic* value of such a wealth tax would be instrumental in educating whites about the systemic injustice of apartheid. The last paragraph of my testimony reads as follows: 'Greater knowledge and a better *understanding of the systemic injustices* – that have been part and parcel of the South African system for at least 100 years – are necessary to succeed with a programme of white *adult education* about the true nature of twentieth-century events, something highly needed *en route* towards a durable reconciliation. Without a clear *understanding* of the *systemic* nature of the *exploitation* that has taken place, it would also not be possible for the beneficiaries (i.e. mainly whites) to make the necessary *confession*, to show the necessary *repentance*, to experience the necessary *conversion* and to be prepared to make the needed *sacrifices*. Confession, repentance, conversion and sacrifices are not only prerequisite for forgiveness (by the victims), but also a precondition for promoting *social stability* and *systemic* justice in the long run. Social stability and systemic justice are, in their turn, preconditions for economic growth and job creation'. Both the corporate sector and the ANC government rejected my proposal for a wealth tax as unrealistic and not implementable. At the time when I gave evidence before the TRC, I was not aware of the elite compromise between the MEC and the ANC that had already excluded a comprehensive redistribution policy as part of the ANC's policy agenda. Several persons have told me

recently that it is a pity that my proposal for a wealth tax was not accepted in 1997.

[26] When permission was granted by big corporations to shift their main listings to London and New York, the corporations promised the ANC government that they would, in their capacity as global corporations, be in a position to mobilise and to redirect much more foreign direct investment to South Africa. Nothing came of those lofty promises. On the contrary, these corporations' shift to foreign stock markets led to a large outflow of long-term capital.

[27] It must be emphasised that the Truth and Reconciliation Commission was very critical of the evidence the Anglo-American Corporation and the Chamber of Mines delivered before it. Unfortunately, the TRC criticised the AAC and the Chamber of Mines only for the untrustworthiness of their evidence and not for the systemic exploitation that had been committed by them over a period of 100 years (TRC 1998).

[28] In 2009 Prof. Mahmood Mamdani (of Columbia University in New York), Prof. Drucilla Cornell (of Rutgers University in the US) and I issued a declaration in which we request that a commission of justice and reconciliation should be appointed to make a proper investigation into the systemic exploitation that took place from the time of the Mineral Revolution (in 1886) until the end of apartheid in 1994.

[29] I was a member of the commission of inquiry into matters concerning the coloured population group (the Theron Commission) from 1973 until 1976. The coloured population group was at that time less than 2 million people. The Commission came to the conclusion that 40 per cent of them (or 800 000 people) were living in chronic community poverty that was perpetuated systemically from one generation to another. The coloured community is presently 4,5

million of which 1,3 million (or 30 per cent) are among the poorest 25 million South Africans. It is depressing that they have made so little progress over the past thirty-six years.

[30] Nef and Reiter (2009: 110) describe the incapacity of the poor as follows: 'Poverty is not a question of material deprivation and limited accessibility to wealth and opportunity. It is essentially a multisided problem of disenfranchisement and exclusion, generally vested in powerlessness and exploitation. Ultimately, it is sanctioned by force. This state of insecurity and 'ill-being' juxtaposes material want with numerous socio-economic, cultural and political circumstances. These reinforce and maintain people in a vulnerable and demeaned condition of unsustainable livelihood, where political, economic and social insecurities are closely interconnected'.

[31] Amartya Sen (2009: chapter 15) emphasises the role public reasoning plays in a well-functioning democracy. The poor are clearly not in a position to participate effectively in public reasoning.

[32] The United Democratic Front (UDF) is the best example of a fairly effective civil society organisation that was abolished un-necessarily by the ANC. After the struggle foreign donor funds were either completely suspended or redirected by the ANC. This created a crisis of survival for many civil society groups. While the different churches played an important civil society role during the struggle, many of them have been co-opted into service delivery projects by the government. The inability of the churches to stop the ANC from declining from an organization with high moral standards into an irresponsible and immoral organisation must be deplored. We certainly could have expected of the churches – given their close cooperation with the ANC during the struggle – to have done much more to denounce the ANC government for neglecting the poor so obviously.

Chapter five

[33] In terms of budgetary spending, South Africa is amongst the top 30 countries in the world, but as far as 'output' is concerned, South Africa is among the lowest 10 out of 140 countries.

Chapter six

[34] Prof Ashwin Desai (2006), alleges that the ANC labour legislation has not succeeded in abolishing the migrant labour system. 'As for the abolition of migrant labour the ANC once again focuses on form rather than content. Property relations, job opportunities and industrial strategy all conspire to have the migrant worker still very much among us, not housed in barracks or Bantustans, but in the squalid *mjondolos* (shack settlements) on the outskirts of our cities'.

[35] Immediately before the Anglo-Boer War started, on 11 October 1899, the Transvaal government published a little book, *'Het eeu van Onreg'* (The century of injustice). The purpose of the book was to emphasise the unjust way the colonial government in Britain treated the Boers in the Transvaal.

[36] According to Credit Suisse there are an estimated 71 000 dollar-millionaires in South Africa (Die Burger 15/03/2012).

Bibliography

Arrighi, G 1994. *The Long Twentieth Century.* London: Verso.

Arrighi, G 2007. *Adam Smith in Beijing, Lineages of the Twenty-first Century.* London: Verso.

Ashman, S; Fine, B and Newman, S (eds) 2011. The crisis in South Africa: neoliberalism, financialisation and uneven and combined development. *Social Register*, 2011.

Bairoch, P, 1982, 'International Industrialization Levels from 1750 to 1980' in *Journal of European Economic History*, 11. 1982.

Bairoch, P, 1993, *Economics and World History, Myths and Paradoxes*, Chicago, The University and Chicago Press.

Blaut, J M 2000. *Eight Eurocentric Historians.* New York: The Guildford Press.

Boxer, CR 1966. *The Dutch Seaborne Empire: 1600-1800.* London: Hutchinson.

Braudel, F 1977. *Afterthoughts on Material Civilisation and Capitalism.* Baltimore MD: Johns Hopkins University Press.

Burbank, J and Cooper, F 2010. *Empires in World History.* Princeton: Princeton University Press.

Colás, A and Saull, R (eds) 2006. *The War on Terror and American 'Empire' after the Cold War.* London: Routledge.

Commission for Employment Equity (CEC) 2011. *Annual Report.*

Cornell, D and Pafilio, KM 2010. *Symbolic Forms for a New Humanity.* New York: Fordham University Press.

Cornia, G et al 2004. *Inequality, Growth and Poverty in the Era of Liberalisation and Globalisation, Oxford: Oxford University Press.*

Cronin, Jeremy 2005. The people shall govern – class struggles and the post 1994 in South Africa (unpublished).

De Gracia, V 2005. *Irresistible Empire, America's Advance through Twentieth Century Europe.* London: The Belknap Press.

Desai, Ashwin 2006. Bend it like the SACP? Or is this treason? (unpublished).

Development Bank of Southern Africa 2008. Economic and Social Infrastructure in South Africa, Infrastructure Barometer.

Dupper, Ockert 2008. Affirmative action: who, how and how long. *South African Journal on Human Rights*, 24.

Edigheji, Omano 2007. A*ffirmative Action and State Capacity in a Democratic South Africa.* Johannesburg: Centre for Policy Studies.

Employment Equity Act 1998 (Act 55 of 1998).

Fine, B and Rustomjee, Z 1996. *The Political Economy of South Africa. From Minerals-Energy Complex to Industrialisation.* Johannesurg: Witwatersrand University Press.

Hedetoft, U 2009. Globalisation and United States empire: moments in the forging of the global turn. In Streeter, Stephen et al 2001. *Empires and Autonomy.* Toronto: UBC Press.

Howe, S 2002. *Empire – A Very Short Introduction.* Oxford: Oxford University Press.

Johnson, C 2004. *The Sorrows of Empire: Militarism, Secrecy and the End of the Republic.* London: Verso.

Kennedy, P 1988. *The Rise and Fall of the Great Powers.* London: Unwin Hyman.

Leibrant, M; Woolard, I; McEvan, H and Koep, C 2011. *Employment and Inequality Outcomes in South Africa.* Cape Town: SALDRU, University of Cape Town.

Leibrant, M and Woolard, I 2010. *Trends in Inequality and Poverty over the Post-apartheid Era: What Kind of Society is Emerging.* Cape Town: SALDRU, University of Cape Town.

Maddison, A 2007. *Contours of the World Economy, 1 – 2030 AD.* Oxford: Oxford University Press.

Mosoetsa, S 2011. *Eating From One Pot.* Johannesburg: Wits University Press.

Mbeki, M 2009. *Architects of Poverty: Why African Capitalism Needs Changing.* Johannesburg: Picador Africa.

Münkler, H 2007. E*mpires – The logic of World Domination from Ancient Rome to the United States Policy.*

National Planning Commission 2011. *National Development Plan.*

Nef, J and Reiter, J 2009. *The Democratic Challenge.* Basingstoke: Palgrave Macmillan.

Okun, Ather, 1975, E*quality and Efficiency – The Big Trade-off,* Washinton, The Brookings Institute.

O'Meara, D 1995. *Forty Lost Years.* Randburg: Ravan.

Sadie, JL 1991. *The South African Labour Force, 1960-2005.* Navorsingsverslag 178. Pretoria: Buro van Marknavorsing, Unisa.

Sen, Amartya 2006. *Identity and Violence: The Illusion of Destiny.* London: Allen Lane.

Stiglitz, J 2002 *Globalization and its Discontents,* London, Allen Lane.

Stiglitz, J 2003 *The Roaring Nineties,* London, Allen Lane.

Streeter, S J and Coleman W (eds) 2009. *Empires and Autonomy.* Toronto: UBC Press.

Terreblanche, *SJ 2002. The History of Inequality in South Africa: 1652- 2002.* Pietermaritzburg: University of Natal Press.

Truth and Reconciliation Commission of South Africa Report: 1988, Vol. 4. Cape Town: Caxton Press.

Van der Westhuizen, C 2007. *White Power, and the rise and Fall of the National Party.* Johannesburg: Zebra Press.

White Paper: Affirmative Action in the Public Service, Government Gazette, Vol. 394, No. 18800, 1998.